Your Diamond Dreams Cut Open My Arteries

UNC | COLLEGE OF ARTS AND SCIENCES
Germanic and Slavic Languages and Literatures

From 1949 to 2004, UNC Press and the UNC Department of Germanic & Slavic Languages and Literatures published the UNC Studies in the Germanic Languages and Literatures series. Monographs, anthologies, and critical editions in the series covered an array of topics including medieval and modern literature, theater, linguistics, philology, onomastics, and the history of ideas. Through the generous support of the National Endowment for the Humanities and the Andrew W. Mellon Foundation, books in the series have been reissued in new paperback and open access digital editions. For a complete list of books visit www.uncpress.org.

Your Diamond Dreams Cut Open My Arteries
Poems by Else Lasker-Schüler

TRANSLATED AND WITH AN INTRODUCTION

BY ROBERT P. NEWTON

UNC Studies in the Germanic Languages and Literatures
Number 100

Copyright © 1982

This work is licensed under a Creative Commons CC BY-NC-ND license. To view a copy of the license, visit http://creativecommons.org/licenses.

Suggested citation: Lasker-Schüler, Else. *Your Diamond Dreams Cut Open My Arteries: Poems by Else Lasker-Schüler.* Translated by Robert P. Newton. Chapel Hill: University of North Carolina Press, 1982. DOI: https://doi.org/ 10.5149/9781469656670_Lasker-Schuler

Library of Congress Cataloging-in-Publication Data
Names: Newton, Robert P.
Title: Your diamond dreams cut open my arteries : Poems by Else Lasker-Schüler / by Robert P. Newton.
Other titles: University of North Carolina Studies in the Germanic Languages and Literatures ; no. 100.
Description: Chapel Hill : University of North Carolina Press, [1982] Series: University of North Carolina Studies in the Germanic Languages and Literatures. | Includes bibliographical references and index.
Identifiers: LCCN 82002656 | ISBN 978-1-4696-5666-3 (pbk: alk. paper) | ISBN 978-1-4696-5667-0 (ebook)
Subjects: Lasker-Schüler, Else, 1869-1945 — Translations into English.
Classification: LCC PT2623.A76 A26 1982 | DCC 831/ .912

Contents

Else Lasker-Schüler	3
Notes	51
Poems from Books and Poem Cycles	
Styx (1902)	56
The Seventh Day (1905)	106
My Miracles (1911)	130
To My So Beloved Playmate Senna Hoy (1917)	146
To My Pure Friend in Love Hans Ehrenbaum-Degele (1917)	158
Gottfried Benn (1917)	162
Hans Adalbert von Maltzahn (1917)	184
My Pretty Mother Always Looked to Venice (1917)	236
Hebrew Ballads (1913)	244
Concert (1932)	264
My Blue Piano (1945)	274
To Him (1945)	290
Identifications	305
Bibliography	307
Index of Poem Titles	313
Subject Index	315

Acknowledgments

Acknowledgment is made to Kösel-Verlag, Munich, for
permission to translate the poems in this book.
Thanks are due to Inter Nationes, Bonn,
and to the Research Council of the
University of North Carolina at Greensboro
for grants to aid in the preparation
of this work.

Robert P. Newton

Your Diamond Dreams
Cut Open My Arteries

Else Lasker-Schüler

1.

A bulky American desk encyclopedia, undoubtedly an arbiter and repository of only the most worthwhile information, cannot find room for her slender figure between Lasker, Emanuel: German chess player and mathematician, and Laski, Harold Joseph: English political scientist, economist, author, and lecturer.

The *Kleines literarisches Lexikon*, in its 1953 edition, eight years after her death, gives as a capsule orientation the following message:

> Lasker-Schüler, Else, lyricist, in themes, ethos, and style an Expressionist. Also stories & dr. 1876–1945,* in Elberfeld,† in Jerusalem. Strongly improvisatory talent, alternating between pure poetry and unrestrained fancifulness. Drawn to the Orient and Judaism as if by mythical memory. Close friendship with Peter→Hille, championed by Karl→Kraus, associations with→ Däubler,→Trakl, Franz Marc. Lived a bohemian life usually in Berlin. 1933 emigration to Switzerland and Palestine.[1]

The missing listing in the encyclopedia is not surprising, for Lasker-Schüler is almost unknown in the English-speaking world and until recently has remained largely untranslated.

But even the sober, telegraphic report of the German lexicon, in itself not incorrect (save in the birth date), could hardly convey to a user the impression that she had also evoked judgments such as these:

> This was the greatest woman poet that Germany ever had.[2]

> Perhaps the greatest poet the Jews have ever had.[3]

> Her poetry . . . belongs, in the development of modern European poetry since Baudelaire, since the French symbolists, among the highest achievements.[4]

> The Black Swan of Israel.[5]

> In a time in which it became difficult and rare or intolerable and conventional, she brought the love song, the love poem once more to great beauty.[6]

> A body of love poetry that is remarkable for its wealth, its variety of nuances and its power.[7]

> Some of the most beautiful love songs that German literature possesses.[8]
>
> She is the Sappho of our century, a "black Sappho," for whom the world has split apart.[9]

The Sappho of our century would probably not have wanted to appear among chess players and political scientists anyway. She was sensitive—hypersensitive—to the company she kept. And, incidentally, she had good reason to be cautious. Not everyone was a friend, as the following charges indicate:

> An extravagant unartistic style is characteristic of her, also a gypsy-like erotic sensibility. Her poetry seems more calculated and artificial than original.[10]
>
> This in part perverse poetry.[11]
>
> A boundlessly egoistic spirit addicted to play.[12]
>
> A pathological urge to lie.[13]
>
> One can doubt that Else Lasker-Schüler was ever psychologically healthy.[14]
>
> A public danger, mentally ill.[15]
>
> Total softening of the brain, we hear the reader say.[16]

Lasker-Schüler was described at various periods of her life as a mixture of archangel and market peddler[17] or witch,[18] as a strayed bird of paradise,[19] a giggling elf or fortune-telling herbwoman,[20] an inextricable chaos of genius and craziness, of megalomania and intentional eccentricity.[21] Of her own changeable nature Lasker-Schüler said: "I'm not a human being, I'm weather."[22]

Artists, by the very nature of their role as forces of the spirit, arouse strong sympathies in their disciples and rejection by their antagonists, but the tone of the reactions to Else Lasker-Schüler is more personal than is usual. With her flagrant eccentricities and aggressive frankness she was hard for her contemporaries to ignore, and she appears to still evoke passions and prejudices in more recent critics. Though she was given to personal devotedness, infatuations, and friendships, the emotional demands she made on others as well as on herself often strained or broke the very bonds with which she sought to secure herself in the void of her lifelong loneliness.

Because her own nature was divided, it is understandable that her critical image is not yet firmly fixed. Indeed, the existential fascination of her work, apart from the great beauty of language and music in a number of poems, lies in following the plight of a self-obsessed soul, threatened every moment with the loss of self, striving to find a saving union with others but always fearing its own dissolution in nothingness, the fading away of that sense of a unique being which was all it had. (Note the number of poems in the Index that begin with the word "My.") After a youth dedicated to considerable self-dramatization, so much a part of her nature that it never ceased, she faced in middle life the ominous eclipse of feeling's warmth, the petrifaction of her kaleidoscopic consciousness. She lived on then in the sustaining hope that her true and unknown essence would someday reveal itself:

> I used to be an actress; now I sit in the cloakroom and burn the audience's straw hats and coats. Because I'm disappointed. I was always seeking a hand, and what lay in my hand—if I was lucky—? a glove. My face is like stone now; I have trouble moving it. One should be proud of that; no one has to erect a monument to you any longer. If only they would decorate me, at least on holidays. The more afraid I am, the more enormous my fearlessness grows. But I'm always afraid; a bird is fluttering somewhere in me, can't take flight any longer. . . . Perhaps it will begin to sing tomorrow. All my life I've been waiting for this song.[23]

The feelings of isolation, abandonment, and disillusion are clear, as is, in the context, the immediate source of her dejection; the passage stems from the same "letter" to Franz Marc (in *The Malik*) where she announces that the love of the poet Gottfried Benn for her has been extinguished.

And yet her capacity for self-identification with other beautiful souls rejuvenated quickly throughout her life—her feelings for Benn never cooled completely—and in late 1913 and 1914, only a year after the above letter, we find her involved in the fate of one of those colorful figures to whom she was always drawn and who were perhaps indeed (how can we honestly know at this remove?) somewhat as admirable and saintly as she found them.

It was a scene worthy both of her penchant for the theatrical and of the power of her loyalty:

> At the end he lay in the Prisoners' Section of the Insane Asylum in Meshcherskoye four hours from Moscow. I had as I entered no longer complete control of myself. We first had to go through 8

towers his brother and I high up between the walls. In front
of every gate of the tower stood 8 armed soldiers or guards. Next
to his cell (he lay with 104 degree fever pneumonia on a *dreadful* bed) raged insane convicts. Please don't take it as sentimentality on the wall hung my picture quite alone. He lay there worthy
of adoration without complaint only a king. I was compelled to
continuously kiss his hands; the kiss that he gave me on my
brow is the most unforgettable blessing that could ever fall
to my lot. I can't write only stammer these events for five
pages.[24]

Five pages, moreover, of her typically self-reliant punctuation.

The prisoner Johannes Holzmann, whose given name Lasker-Schüler had reversed in its order of letters to read "Senna Hoy" (see the lyrics dedicated to him, also called "Sascha"), had been, in the years around 1904, the editor of a periodical in Berlin entitled *Kampf* ("Struggle"). Subsequently, his anarchistic politics and indignation at Slavic pogroms lured him to Imperial Russia, still a stronghold of reaction, where he was arrested, accused of subversive activities, and sentenced in 1907 to fifteen years of forced labor. Eight years he spent imprisoned in Warsaw and Moscow; under confinement he became mentally ill, made several suicide attempts, and finally died under the circumstances depicted above. Lasker-Schüler's appearance at the site of his Russian confinement was in pursuit of her and his brother's efforts to have Holzmann released, a man whose honesty, piety toward mankind, loneliness, and greatness she worshiped almost like a saint's, and apparently quite platonically: "They all pushed themselves on him, he was so beautiful that he was without will-power in love, I mean a work of art that can't defend itself, that one should leave untouched just for that reason. I always had an ascetic relationship with him."[25]

Despite approaches to and promises of help given by highly placed personages at the Russian Court, these efforts for Holzmann's release proved in vain because of the German Embassy's clear wish to prevent his return to Germany. It expressed the fear that he might make an attempt on the Emperor's life. After the death of Lasker-Schüler's friend, his body was sent back to Berlin, where she attended the funeral: "There is something more grandiose than love, he was the person most dear to me; every shovel-full of earth that fell on his coffin also fell on my face. I felt the joy of violence, as if one were beating oneself on the face."[26]

The whole episode of Senna Hoy, occurring in the feverish last half year before the outbreak of World War I, shows Else Lasker-Schüler in an atypically active relationship to the "real" world, and, perhaps for that reason, in an apocalyptic mood; for the year 1914 marked a turning point in her own life also, a loss of many friends to the war, a hiatus in her productive powers. Like the ill-fated arch-expressionists Heym, Trakl, van Hoddis, and others, she scented disaster in the air and seemed to long for it: "A wave is always pounding on my heart, I always have to cross God's grave. I almost think he's dead and the Bible is his gravestone. For human feelings it can only seem like willfulness—if he's alive and has turned away. I'm completely God-forsaken or pinched in between his intestines. I wish there would be a great fire. House after house should burn; I'm all aflame to ignite the entire Kurfürstendamm."[27]

An Else Lasker-Schüler traveling to Moscow to negotiate with ministers of state for a friend embroiled in the imperial political labyrinths, a Lasker-Schüler invoking a vast conflagration in Berlin, her succoring cultural milieu, is a rather different Lasker-Schüler from the one customarily portrayed in bohemian dress and eccentric habit, rapidly passing through exalted affections of the heart. These latter facets of her life—often accentuated and hard to ignore—tend to mask the powerful poet who, despite her illusions and fantasy selves as Tino of Baghdad or the Prince of Thebes, was gifted with acute psychological insight, surprisingly frequent common sense, and, essential for a poet, a readiness to accept her feelings unreservedly.

In addition, though Lasker-Schüler was no intellectual, her work obviously reflects many of the problems of modern consciousness, such as the enfeebling dispersal of the central self, its alienation from the communal soul, and its radical disorientation through the loss of fixed beliefs. Though not a thinker, she held and she lived out a view of life as feeling, spontaneity, and the search for community with the world.

2.

On reality's stage Else Lasker-Schüler was a small and slender woman with a boyish figure, large, gleaming eyes—"Spanish" and "unforgettable"—with hair worn short, a style that at the turn of the century was for a woman an attention-getter. This, of course, she welcomed. Her sense of humor and the ridiculous was marked. Her gaze was penetrating but evasive; in later years she could look angry, but as a younger woman, with her comely face and extravagant mannerisms, she exerted considerable fascination, even—or especially—on the gaping bourgeois youth who admired the freedoms she permitted herself. She dressed in a fashion likely to irritate the lovers of good order: unmatching blouse and skirt, red velvet jacket with golden buttons, Turkish pants and boots, a fur-piece in the summer, a jockey's cap on her raven locks. As she grew older the charm of her embellishments may have seemed less appropriate. Armin T. Wegner, otherwise quite prepossessed with the poetess, describes her appearance as that of "a no longer young oriental daughter of joy."[28]

Perhaps the liveliest conjuration of her person is that of Gottfried Benn, himself a leading poet of their generation, by nature more intellectual than spontaneous, to whom for a short while Lasker-Schüler was romantically attached and who maintained a relationship of respect and admiration for her until her death:

> Neither then nor later could one even cross the street with her without all the world standing still and looking at her: extravagant wide skirts or pants, impossible upper garments, neck and arms decked with showy imitation jewelry, chains, earrings, fake golden rings on her fingers, and since she was continuously stroking strands of hair out of her face, these—one must admit it—servant girl's rings were always at the center of everyone's gaze. She never ate regularly, she ate very little, often she lived for weeks on nuts and fruits. She often slept on benches, and she was always poor at all times and in all stages of her life. This was the Prince of Thebes, Jussuf, Tino of Baghdad, the Black Swan.
> And this was the greatest woman poet that Germany ever had.[29]

Yes, she was indeed eccentric, perhaps obsessed; her friends admitted it and remained loyal. In part she was eccentric from inner compulsion; her father, for example, had had no high opinion of girls, whence probably the haircut, pants, and cap, a guise she adopted in part as a young girl.[30] But the eccentricity also was a form of self-stylization or mythification, the outer manifestation of the fictional personalities she adopted, a flag of the rejection of "life" in favor of "art" in the neoromantic sense of Thomas Mann's *Tonio Kröger*.

Beyond all this, though, she was indeed profoundly odd. For example, she claimed quite seriously that she was visited by spirits: young King David, the Angel Gabriel, her deceased grandfather. She warned people next to her table at the Café of the West not to step on the toes of Achmed, her black servant, supposedly standing beside her but invisible to all others.[31] In the broad daylight of Berlin she once experienced her own transformation into a negroid being from primordial times, with six arms, on whose body was printed a message in an unknown alphabet.[32]

These visions sometimes help to explain cryptic images in the poetry. In "Leave Taking" she says her heart "hangs on every doorpost," a curious association that recurs to a childhood apparition: her heart, dark red, hanging for seconds on the doorpost of her playroom, a hallucination that, when reported to her mother, caused the latter considerable apprehension.[33]

It is not surprising that some prosaic critics doubted her sanity or suspected her of self-promotion, a motivation, it must be said, of which she was not completely unaware. Some of her apparent peculiarity, however, was no more than a total frankness of expression, something we—and certainly Wilhelminian Germany—are not accustomed to. She purportedly told the dramatist Gerhart Hauptmann to his face that he looked like Goethe's grandmother. (Was she so wrong?)[34] She forced one couple in an audience to leave the hall before she began one of her poetry readings, since she could not tolerate their baleful "emanations."[35] And she returned from another recital to report with horror that it was attended by three hundred butcher's apprentices, each with a sharpened knife in hand, which may well have described the case metaphorically.[36]

It is difficult, from a distance, to resist the grotesque charm of her fancy, not to be bemused by the pride of self-significance revealed in such anecdotes, and no one reporting on or explicating Else Lasker-Schüler can repress the urge to cite them. But without the wealth of her poetry she would simply be another of the numerous bohemian ladies-errant of the times, about whom entertaining tales are rife. One might mention Emmy Hennings in this connection, an actress and poetess, who turned streetwalker for a while, and who under a friend's assumed identity served the latter's sentence in jail, since the friend at the time had a conflicting theater job. (Hennings later married Hugo Ball of Dadaist fame, a congenerous madcap.) And then there was Bettina Jacometti, Dutch, a gifted artist and pupil of Aubrey Beardsley, who served some time in the French Foreign Legion without being detected as a woman.[37] In the hothouse aesthetic culture of the times the exotics flourished.

With Else Lasker-Schüler the oddities begin to make sense when we pick up her poetry, where the masks are largely stripped away and in the best of which her truthfulness to human feeling and her self-created myth become one. We then begin to see her early erotic lyrics, her deeper devotional love poetry, the poems to her son, her effusions of melancholy and ardent religious invocations, we begin to see these all as expressions of an emotional dilemma, as a longing for close contact, to be sure, but also as a desire for complete freedom. From this dilemma the legendary identities she has assumed represent but a vehicle of escape.

In her deepest nature she remained unaffectedly childlike, a "primordial child" (*Urkind*), as she called her friend Peter Hille. A decent person, she said, should remain a schoolchild all his life.[38] A child is playfully open to experience but easily disappointed, is dependent on the love of others but unable to recognize their own claims to attention, and does not acknowledge the advance of time or any provident seriousness beyond the moment. Lasker-Schüler confessed: "I make an effort; but I can only play, in writing too."[39] The game of writing poems she compares with her laying out of rows of multicolored buttons, a favorite pastime as a child.

Her often lonely and vagabond existence, although subconsciously self-chosen, afforded the freedom of childhood as long as she also accepted its helplessness and poverty, but she never overcame her longing for home and familial dependence: "I have no rest, am always unsettled, no home. I wish I were somebody's child. And someone would go with me into all the toy stores and buy me hobbyhorses, little bears, chests full of little houses and trees and sheep and chickens."[40] Her relationship to those she loved, even to God, was often that of a playmate or a sister. (Benn laid special emphasis on her qualities of gratitude, attachment, and limitless loyalty to friends.)[41] And wherever she was, she filled her room with playthings—dolls, animals, tin soldiers posed in battle order. It comes as no surprise that her poems make use of play imagery or that they express boundless enthusiasm for playmate friends and an equally sudden chagrin when the playmates have gone away.

This childlikeness, touching as it might be in modest doses, would soon become tedious if, behind all the games and costumes, there were not a mature and poetic awareness of common joy and sorrow, love and abandonment—one that could clothe itself in innovative, often successfully innovative, language and rhythms.

There is a "sweet and unstillable sadness" pervading her poetry.[42] Taking the phrase from her own work, Gottfried Benn refers to her "unpurposed hand of play and blood" (*ziellose Hand aus Spiel und Blut*),[43] a formula linking her freedom with her instinctual nature. She can be as naïvely uncalculating as a child, but it is a naïveté beyond good and evil that exposes all: "I have confidence in my good and bad actions. I know no sin."[44] And "What I do is well done; I don't doubt myself."[45] Though in fact Lasker-Schüler cannot indefinitely maintain this unquestioning self-confidence (she later often reproached herself for failures in her son's upbringing), there is a sufficiency of it to insure that conventional sentiment will succumb to unflinching honest impulse. An emotion she knows as "falling in love" is an essential force in her life and poetry; yet she does not hesitate to declare on impulse, "I hate and despise mankind without exception."[46]

3.

Shortly before the poetess-to-be celebrated her second birthday, undoubtedly in an atmosphere of affectionate middle-class pomp, the Emperor of the Second German Empire was proclaimed with deadly serious pompousness at captive Versailles on 18 January 1871. It was the beginning of the "founders' age" with its rapid growth of economic prosperity and political ambition in a newly united Germany, a nation of growing pride, of flourishing scientific and cultural activity, but also of developing social problems, worker unrest, and rising tension, where an entrenched authoritarian governing class was forced to confront the opposing claims of the increasingly self-confident laboring and commercial classes. In this multifarious and dynamic but also egoistic and materialist society, artists tended to see one of two paths for their development: either they questioned these trends and viewed the world through magnifying naturalistic glasses, noted in studied detail its sordid imperfections and oppressive forces, siding finally with the social sufferers; or they consciously broke with the "real" world and pursued art as the ultimate goal, as an absolute claim on and animating force of the human spirit. These latter, the champions of aestheticism, were not indifferent to human pain, but they saw art as the possibility of triumph over the world's fatal insufficiency. It is this second path that Else Lasker-Schüler chose to follow. But of course her life was profoundly affected by the world as it rapidly changed, try as she would to ignore the passage of time.

For years her birth date was given as 11 February 1876, the date she adopted at the time of her wedding to Herwarth Walden. Only long after her death was the true year of her birth, 1869, uncovered by Emerich Reeck. Reeck went on to unearth, in a yearbook called *Wer ist's*, a further fictitious birth date promulgated by the poetess, 1881, and Jürgen Wallmann found that in exile in Zurich she had advanced it an additional decade, to 1891, hence claiming herself to be forty-eight at a time when she was already seventy and looked it.[47] Obviously she was more than normally afraid of aging. To attribute this to a "pathological urge to lie," as Reeck does, reveals an almost equally pathological rejection of the role of illusion in her life (and in many other people's lives). Before puncturing Lasker-Schüler's spiritual balloon, what Jung calls psychic inflation, we should reread Ibsen's *Wild Duck* and ask whether accurate records outweigh the productive vital lie.

Among the familial antecedents of Lasker-Schüler were merchants, wine dealers, and bankers; one relative was Leopold Sonnemann, the founder of the *Frankfurter Zeitung*. Her father, Aaron Schüler, was a not unprosperous private banker in Elberfeld, near Wuppertal, whose grandfather had been a rabbi in Gesecke. Aaron Schüler, according to Else's accounts, was a roguishly playful man, given to joking, a town character whose special pleasure lay in "building," probably actually the financing of home construction. At any event, he was not an architect as she claimed. He encouraged his daughter in her dislike of school, preferring to take her to the circus; later, apparently after an injury or illness when she was eleven (she claimed she had jumped from the tower of her house onto an awning), she was tutored at home. From her father she inherited her sense of humor and a considerable talent for drawing, on which she later relied in part for her living and which came to full flower in her son. A picture, fictitious in many respects, is given of her father's family in the story "Arthur Aronymus: The Story of My Father" (1932), as well as in a drama of similar name (1932). Strangely enough, Aaron Schüler does not appear in her poetry at all. But his relationship with her may have disturbed in some way Else's later relationships with other men, as Cohn suggests.[48]

Lasker-Schüler's mother, Jeanette Kissing, was descended ostensibly from a Spanish Jew who had fled a pogrom in Madrid, had gone to England, and later removed to southern Germany, his son adopting there the name of Kissing. This report is given by Else, who depicts her mother as a sensitive and dreamy, refined, somewhat abstracted, and melancholy woman who read a great deal and had literary gifts herself, and who taught her daughter to write. The mother greatly admired figures such as Napoleon, Goethe, and Petöfi, and it was from her that the poetess acquired her proneness to romantic enthusiasms as well as the literary impulse. Jeanette Schüler played a dominant role in her daughter's emotional development and is the subject of a number of poems ("My Quiet Song," "My Mother"). She died when Lasker-Schüler was only twenty-one, but the latter's unstilled longing for her mother's maternal protectiveness and companionship persisted throughout life. "I loved my mother ardently; she was my friend, my icon, my strength, my absolution, my emperor."[49] "I felt like eternal life beside her who had brought me to the world."[50]

There were five children older than Else. She was especially close to and worshipful of her brother Paul, seven years her senior, after whom she later named her only child. He was an imaginative and sympathetic brother, alive to nature and of a religious bent, who, according to Margarete Kupper, had intended to convert to Catholicism but died at the age of twenty-one before doing so.[51] Of the remaining siblings, Anna, the next oldest sister, continued to be the closest to Lasker-Schüler until the former's death in 1912. The poetess seems to have had infrequent contact with the rest of the immediate family in later years, except with Anna's daughters Edda and Erika.

The Schüler household in Elberfeld was a typically bourgeois home of the times, the center of family and social festivities and of cultural interests, untouched by major cares. Lasker-Schüler regarded her youth as a lost paradise of peace and security. She dreamed away her time in school and enjoyed little success, save in religious instruction; even in early years, she tells us, the tale of Joseph and his brothers entranced her. It is part of her self-evolved legend, but confirmed by other sources too,[52] that she avoided reading; at any event, with a few exceptions like Richard Dehmel and Hugo von Hofmannsthal, she seldom comments on other writers. Of course she knew Nietzsche, Däubler, George, to name only a few, but when queried about contemporary authors she typically replied that she knew them personally—why should she read them? "I'm beginning to ask myself whether I'm intellectual or dull,"[53] she says, and, "I personally get headaches from any kind of study. Let one celebrate my ignorance."[54] Yet whatever her mental endowments may in fact have been, she was subject to an overpowering burden of ennui from an early age. As a small child, she writes, she climbed into that same tower of the Schüler house (recent researchers claim the house had no tower)[55] and cried out to the people below, "I'm so bored!"

She was *not* bored as a child by endlessly laying out patterns of colorful buttons and by playing rhyming games with her mother; she hated off-rhymes, she says,[56] though her poems have many. We are informed that she first composed poetry at the age of five,[57] and she afterwards maintained that the poems in her first volume, *Styx*, originated in her fifteenth to seventeenth years.[58]

A cloud of mystery covers the period of her adolescence and young womanhood. In her autobiographical writings Lasker-Schüler is primarily interested in giving the mythical truth of her life, but even in this form she has little to say about these years.

We do know, however, that in 1894, at almost twenty-five, she married Dr. Berthold Lasker, a physician, and moved with him to Berlin, the burgeoning, strident capital of the German Empire. Here she also established a studio for her artistic work. It is with this marriage that her personal destiny begins to unroll. Dr. Lasker seems to have been a rationalistic and ethically rigorous man, hostile to spontaneous love as his wife knew it, a man with whom Else was not happy from the start. He was, incidentally, the brother of that same Emanuel Lasker, world chess champion, mathematician, and philosopher, who managed to win the attention of the desk encyclopedia. The two later coauthored a drama, *The Story of Mankind* (1922).

In September 1899, Lasker-Schüler's son Paul was born, but it was possibly not the son of Berthold Lasker, though he gave it his name. Dieter Bänsch has discovered parallels to this situation in passages from *The Nights of Tino of Baghdad*. If accepted autobiographically, they indicate both that Lasker-Schüler met the child's father in May of 1898 and that her infidelity—which is what she herself claims it was—was sparked by the "blind glances" of her husband and by her own unhappiness with her position as a woman.[59] However, Sigrid Bauschinger surmises that the child may well have been Lasker's and the infidelity another of the poetess's self-invented legends.[60] But, at the time, even a mere hint of suspicion would have been inevitably disruptive because of the rigid Wilhelminian code of honor, however hypocritical that code may have been.

Lasker-Schüler later asserted, in a letter to Karl Kraus, that Paul's father was a Greek named Alcibiades de Rouan. Bänsch, from clues in the work mentioned, believes that he was possibly indeed Greek, but the aristocratic name sounds unconvincing and could easily be a mythical trapping. At any event, the hypothetical Alcibiades de Rouan "died," she claimed, and played no further role in the poetess's life. Her son Paul, however, was from then on the only relatively stable center of her later years. Lasker-Schüler and her husband separated at this point but were not officially divorced until just before her next marriage.

After separation, Else and the child lived for a time in a dungeon-like basement that she rented from a concièrge for 75 pfennigs monthly. From this banishment she was rescued by Peter Hille, one of the first alter egos she literarily enshrined, and by other members of the "New Community" (*Neue Gemeinschaft*), which is described by Bänsch as a "half philosophical, half aesthetic colony of life-reformers, which had become a sort of homeland for Hille and for which Hille was a walking monument. The effect on Else Lasker-Schüler of the programmatic beliefs of this Order of the True Life, so-called by Julius Hart, cannot be overestimated. They simply decreed the inner unity of the self and the world, the vacuity of all opposition as mere conceptual illusion and, conclusively following from that, the power and capacity of human beings to redeem themselves."[61]

Bänsch's work on Lasker-Schüler is motivated by the sociocritical impulse to debunk the progressive beatification of the poetess which had been initiated by some earlier hagiographers; he sees the New Community as a "late bourgeois doctrine of salvation," mingling elements of monism, chiliastic idealism, and the notion of restituting nature's integrity, a doctrine deluded in its "total negation of extrasubjective resisting forces."[62] Obviously such views would be quite compatible with Lasker-Schüler's instinctive tendency to incorporate the world into her ego and would, as well, provide a philosophical justification for her mode of life, including—from the conventional viewpoint—the social shame of her (possible) marital unfaithfulness. The belief in a divine immanence could easily metamorphose into a worshipful devotion to, and identification with, those with whom one fell in love and could spread the warm glow of ontological necessity over what otherwise might seem to be a mere random meeting of empty strangers.

In an essay "The New Man" (1901), a title anticipating expressionist prophecies, Julius Hart expounds: "God is nothing but that which lives, and our *life* is God. By living we do not seek but *are* the truth. For life is all the truth—and in every moment goal and fulfillment."[63] These ideas are clearly reflected even in a quite late essay by Lasker-Schüler, "The Child among the Months," in *Concert*, which offers an uncharacteristically discursive presentation of her religious thought: "I explain to myself God's omnipotence in the world like the mother to the child. . . . We are here to work on the primordial colossus of the world, to empower it, to keep the universe alive, to breathe uninterruptedly. Now insofar as we refined egoists serve the cosmos, we remain alive. Whoever kills himself or his neighbor out of love or enmity becomes a thief of the force of breath that maintains the motion of our Father's created work. My deeply drawn breath unites me with the universe."[64]

This neoromantic mysticism strove to replace the security of traditional faith, which more and more seemed to be a mere historical artifact, by merging the individual with the undifferentiated, encloaking All, a resort perhaps more familiar to some readers in the works of Hermann Hesse (*Siddhartha*, "Klein und Wagner.") With Else Lasker-Schüler, although it persists as a basic inclination, the *unio mystica* is often displaced in her poetry by a more anthropomorphically familial relation to the deity as a playmate, lover, or father. But even this relationship is often weakened by skepticism or an anxious search for the absconded God.

Among the neocommunitarians it was Peter Hille (1854–1904), sometimes dubbed the "Verlaine of Berlin" and a legend in his own right, who replaced for Else her lost brother and mother. Along with their close spiritual affinity as fantasts and eccentrics, the two shared a Westphalian background, though he was Catholic and she Jewish. Gerhart Werner terms Hille a literary gypsy and vagrant, the first hippie of German literature, yet a very prolific writer.[65] A big man with a flowing beard, he wandered through Germany, Italy, and Switzerland, spent two years in London, and was director of a traveling theatrical group in Amsterdam. Through it all he carried with him in brown bags his literary productions—aphorisms, novels (*Semiramis*, *Cleopatra*), rhapsodic poetry—his manuscripts written on odd bits of paper, envelopes, bills, cigarette packs.

Hille was fifteen years older than Lasker-Schüler. Their relationship remained fraternal, but it contained an obvious erotic component that was sublimated into mutual ecstatic admiration. Both lived with the New Community and moved in the artistic circles of the café world. After his untimely death in 1904, she exalted him to the status of a prophet and saint and wrote *The Peter Hille Book* (1906), a mythification of their first encounter and following friendship. Its various legendary personages undoubtedly represent "existences" known to Lasker-Schüler and Hille in the bohemian milieu of Berlin. From this latter-day Saint Peter derives the often-quoted description of Else Lasker-Schüler as "the Black Swan of Israel, a Sappho whose world has split apart. She glows childlike, in primeval darkness."[66] The poetess dedicated the poem "The Fallen Angel" to Peter Hille.

It was Hille who invented Else's first mythical identity as Tino of Baghdad. He also called her "Tino—Queen of the Ultimate Passions," "Dreamtino," and "Mohammed's Wife." She amplified the legend in her book, *The Nights of Tino of Baghdad* (1907), a protracted, orientally lush, and lyrically diffuse fairy tale, which contained in addition a number of her early poems. The first poetry to be published, we should interpolate, had already appeared in 1899 in the periodical *Die Gesellschaft* ("Society"). A first volume of verse, *Styx*, came out in 1902 and a second, *The Seventh Day*, three years later (1905). These poetic works will be discussed separately.

Thus, Else Lasker-Schüler was already a recognized literary figure as well as a personality in café circles when, on 30 November 1903, she entered into her second marriage. Georg Levin was a literatus and composer whom she had met in Hille's social ambient.[67] At the time of the wedding they had already been living together for an unknown period. Taking her cue from Hille's delight in assigning pseudonyms, Lasker-Schüler renamed her husband Herwarth Walden, a cognomen under which he became immortalized in literary histories as the editor, beginning in 1910, of the expressionist periodical *Der Sturm* ("The Storm.") A number of Lasker-Schüler's poems appeared in its pages in 1910 and 1911—actually before the magazine's fully expressionist period, which dates from 1913—but this association accounts for her later being grouped with the expressionist poets, an historical link that is still questionable. One might, of course, point out as common defining features of the poetess and the cultural movement an elevated level of pathos, heightened metaphoricity, experimentation with the forms of language, and freedom of versification; but, as noted before, Lasker-Schüler lacks the utopian world-reforming or apocalyptic impulses of the prototypical expressionists, of the Werfels, Bechers, Heyms, Trakls, Stadlers.

Walden was a hyperactive cultural entrepreneur, always engrossed in new promotions, considered by some to be arrogant and ruthless with his friends. His wife esteemed him highly as a composer, and he set some of her works to music. But, although he spread her literary fame, there were problems in their liaison from the very beginning, and these were not eased by poverty and a nomadically hectic life together. Indications are that, as a divorcée and a woman once involved in an affair, she was not accepted by Levin's family. For her part, she continued to live in her realm of fantasy, while he, in return, was unfaithful with a quite real Swede, a woman he later married. In addition, she worried about the effect of their irregular life on her son Paul. A crisis and separation came in 1910, divorce in 1912. Some writers attribute the breach to his infidelities, others to Else's difficulties with human contact. At any event, the result for Lasker-Schüler was a new traumatic failure in love and a magnified sense of isolation. In spite of this, she often defended Levin in later years in his literary feuds, even against Karl Kraus, an important patron of hers, when the latter attacked *Der Sturm*. Their relationship had been from the first, as Gehlhoff-Claes notes, "a fraternal alliance against the world."[68]

But the time of this personal misalliance was one of creative efflorescence for the writer. *Styx, The Seventh Day, The Peter Hille Book, The Nights of Tino of Baghdad*, and *The Wupper* all appeared in the German bookstores. *The Wupper*, a drama that consists of a balladesque sequence of episodes, is set in her native Wuppertal; it is sometimes naturalistic in language but otherwise lyrically subjective. Poetry written in this period appeared in *My Miracles: Poems* (1911) and in the later *Collected Poems* (1917).

The atmosphere of Lasker-Schüler's life with Levin can be divined in *My Heart: A Love Novel with Pictures and Really Living People* (1912). This "novel" is actually a collection of "letters" to Levin and a friend, ostensibly dispatched while the pair was in Norway but continuing to be conveyed to them through *Der Sturm* even after their return home, an oddity that the authoress herself casually remarks on in the letters. It is, nevertheless, the first of the larger prose works to abandon the fantasies of the *Peter Hille Book* and *Tino of Baghdad* and is interesting both for the vignettes drawn of the poetess's life in Berlin's bohemia and for its personal, religious, and philosophical reflections. Along with stretches of straight reporting—often still in characteristically grotesque romantic metaphors—*My Heart* also introduces the Prince of Thebes, Lasker-Schüler's second mythical personality, who gives the name to another short collection of orientalizing fantasies published in 1914. Further interesting essays, both autobiographical and on literary and artistic figures, were collected in *Visions: Essays and Other Stories* (1913). Lasker-Schüler's nonfantasy prose writings are a profitable source book for the prewar Berlin milieu, as well as a diary of archetypical self-obsession, however flippantly expressed, and they should be taken more seriously than they have been.

After her divorce from Levin, Lasker-Schüler never again had a permanent residence. She lived in hotels and pensions and in the evenings haunted the lively cafés with their marble-topped tables, the Café des Westens and the Romanisches Café, to taste a bit of "objectivity," away from the daze of artistic self-preoccupation that prevailed in her shabbily old-fashioned rented quarters. Upon occasion she was evicted from her café table for failing to place an order, the fate of the perennially penniless. Impractical with money (she usually gave it away as soon as she got it), she was not beyond expressly lusting after it: "If I only had money. Money! Money! Money! Money! . . . "[69] A friend, Katharina Otto, reports that Lasker-Schüler stole a picture by Oskar Kokoschka during a party in an imposing Berlin home, but later she "donated" it to a Kokoschka exhibition.[70] Some income was produced by her books, though she felt cheated by her publishers, one and all, and attacked them vivaciously in *Cleaning Out!* (*Ich räume auf!* 1925). She slapped a publisher once in the foyer of a theater and claimed her hand was guided by an archangel.[71] More income derived, however, from articles and public readings of her poetry (in extravagant "oriental" costume, with flutes and bells), performed in Kurt Hiller's Neopathetic Cabaret and in Munich, Zurich, Vienna, Cologne, Dresden, Königsberg, and Prague. In Prague she was arrested for disturbing the peace while orating "in the Arabian language" about her destiny to twenty-five companions from a "niche" of the cathedral. But, even in sum, these activities could barely support her. The well-disposed critic Karl Kraus solicited contributions for her through his periodical *Die Fackel* ("The Torch") in 1913, and a helpful amount was forthcoming, showing that her art—which after all was her saving raison d'être—had not gone unnoticed.

But she was not happy, as we read in her letters to Karl Kraus. She felt her life was loathsome, ruined, a failure; she was "so alone." The brighter moments were due to her friends and her young son Paul.

Paul, who was the subject of a number of her poems and whose death at twenty-seven occasioned her beautiful "To My Child," was a gifted boy in whom she saw blossoming everything that was blurred and withered in herself.[72] Her claims for his beauty, charm, and early talent are confirmed by others; he was, for her, kissed by "a breath from the Gods" ("My Child"). She admired his truly "artistic," i.e., not "intellectual," nature, his roguish playfulness, and his scorn for everything pretentious. Like her, she felt, he was seeking happiness and the miracle of love; he was not only her son but also her little brother, "the person with whom she could always communicate without difficulty" (Gehlhoff).[73] As a boy she took him with her on Sunday afternoons to the Café of the West, where he sat quietly at one of the marble tables behind the steps and drew. His youthful artistic talent was apparently genuine and was recognized not only by academic artists but also, among others, by Franz Marc, the expressionist painter of "Blue Horse" fame. A friend of Lasker-Schüler who died in the war, Hans Ehrenbaum-Degele (coeditor with Paul Zech of *Das neue Pathos*, "The New Pathos"; see the poems dedicated to him) left money in his will to further Paul's training. Lasker-Schüler never ceased to blame herself for not providing properly for him. Although her poems to him suggest a playful, loving, and attentive parent ("The Baboon Mother"), she could not or would not be other than she was, and it was almost inevitable that he enter the same vagabondage as his poet-mother; she saw in him an "enchanting Don Juan, seeking the one and only."[74] According to Bauschinger, his later work did not live up to his early promise.[75]

Lasker-Schüler seems to have had, as Hans Cohn puts it, "a gift for making friends and also for antagonizing them." Cohn goes on to say: "Whatever the fate of her relationships, some of her most successful poems are penetrating evocations of the personalities of her friends, most of them artists and writers. These poems are 'objective' in the sense . . . [that] the poet's feelings about people she knew and loved have crystallized into poetic portraits of great insight and precision."[76] We can assume these friendships were genuine—many, men and women, displayed their loyalty to the poetess before and after her death—but that need not mean that unrelieved contact with Lasker-Schüler was easy or that the romantic cast of many poems of friendship reflects, in every case, a serious, long-term attachment. To call it an erotically tinged affection might, in most cases, be closer to the mark.

Her worshipful friendship with the imprisoned radical Johannes Holzmann, who, like Peter Hille, served as a brother-surrogate, falls in the period between her second divorce and World War I. Her Platonic but strong and lasting links to him, as well as his unhappy end, were depicted at the outset of this Introduction. To him are dedicated the poems "Ballad," "My Love Song," "A Love Song," "A Song of Love," none of which reflects an actual erotic relationship, and also "Senna Hoy" and "Sascha," with its pensive lines: "Strange that we never kissed/Our whole life long" (which seems to describe more accurately how things stood, according to her letter to Karl Kraus). Even in death, Johannes was her guardian angel ("Senna Hoy"), interposed reassuringly between her and the terror of dying. The verses: "And I am incomprehensible to our friends/And become a stranger" (since his passing), suggest that Holzmann, like Hille before him, provided social mediation between Lasker-Schüler and a world of less beatific acquaintances.

Karl Kraus, the Viennese author and critic, was the friend most helpful to Lasker-Schüler's career. They were, of course, not in daily contact but corresponded rather frequently between 1909 and 1923; in her letters she addressed him variously as the "Cardinal," the "Dalai

Lama," and the "Duke of Vienna," and she reveals a surprising "career consciousness."

Kraus published some of her poetry in *Die Fackel*, a periodical influential in literary circles. He called her a "great poet" and in particular praised her poem "An Old Tibetan Rug," a poem that, he said, "belongs for me to the most enchanting and touching I have ever read. And there are few from Goethe on down in which, as in this Tibetan Rug, sense and sound, word and image, language and soul are so interwoven."[77]

On two occasions when the poetess was in financial straits (1913 and 1925), Kraus appealed with success for contributions from his readers, and in general he seemed to serve in the office of father confessor, at least from Else's point of view. But their friendship foundered on Lasker-Schüler's maternal pride and, she would have said, on the critic's lack of "heartfeltness" (*Innigkeit*); specifically, she was mortally offended that Kraus had not invited her son Paul to visit while the latter was sojourning in Vienna. The final words in her last letter to Kraus during the period of their closeness were: "I hate you."

Perhaps her most famous friend or beloved was the poet-doctor Gottfried Benn, who came on stage with the restive expressionist generation, flirted briefly with the radical conservatism of the 1930s until disillusioned by the National Socialists, and then resurfaced after World War II as the doyen of modernist poets. His early work, fusing the aesthetics of ugliness with a cool, nihilistic intellectuality, could hardly seem further removed from the ardent impetuosity of Else Lasker-Schüler. But moments of despair and alienation were also not unknown to her, and she undoubtedly admired his somber, unflinching gaze and his courage in ignoring poetic convention: "He descends into the vaults of his hospital and dissects the dead. Insatiable to enrich himself with mystery. . . . Long before I knew him I was his reader; his volume of poems—*Morgue*—lay on my blanket: horrible miracles of art, reveries of death, that assumed contour. Sufferings gape their maws and are silent, cemeteries wander into the sick-wards and take up position before the beds of pain. Women in childbirth one hears screaming from the delivery room, on to the end of the world. Each of his verses a leopard bite, the spring of a savage animal. Bone is his stylus, with which he resurrects the word."[78]

They met in 1912, and the "affair" was actually a brief one, ending probably in 1913.[79] Though she seems to have fallen passionately in love with Benn, his feelings were less strong, but he always remained a loyal admirer of her personally and of her work. Her, as usual rather extravagant sentiments are described in *The Malik: An Imperial Story* (1919), a series of letters to Franz Marc: "I have indeed fallen in love again. Even if I fell in love a thousand times, it is always a new miracle; [whereas it's just] the old nature of things, when someone else falls in love.... His brain is a lighthouse. He is one of the Nibelungs."[80]

Yet in the very next letter she must regret the fading of his love, and she then lapses into a vein of desolation, proclaiming herself tired of life, both bored and fearful, loving no one in the world anymore. This is the same letter from which we earlier quoted the passage: "My face is now like stone, I have trouble moving it."[81]

The real fruits of this adventure were the numerous poems dedicated to Giselheer the Barbarian, namely Benn: "Oh, Your Hands," "To Giselheer the Heathen," "Pure Diamond," "The Song of the Playmate Prince," "I Hide behind Trees," "To Giselheer the Tiger," "O God," "Listen," "Turned Inward," "Only for You," and "To the Barbarian." These poems reveal in turn her passion, her affection and quiet devotion, her uncertainty and disappointment, and her ultimate forsakenness. Clemens Heselhaus has observed that in the poetry written to Benn the "tone is much more personal than in the other dedicatory poems. The literary allusions are abandoned. Only after being separated from Benn does she return to her orientalizing metaphors and emblems."[82] In the poems to Benn we find some of her strongest and most original love poetry.

The encounter was not without lasting effect for Benn also. It has been suggested by F. W. Wodtke that Benn's poems "Ein Mann spricht," "Drohung," and "Madonna" were influenced by Lasker-Schüler's work, as is evidenced by their surrealistically visionary language and imagery and, one might add, by their rhythms.[83] Benn's second volume of poetry, *Söhne* (*Sons*, 1914), is dedicated to her. But the most direct response is found in Benn's poem "Hier ist kein Trost" ("No Solace Here"), which, with its beginning verses, "No one will be my road's edge./Let your blossoms fade away./My road streams and goes alone," is a stern reply to Lasker-Schüler's "Listen": "I am your road's edge./She that skirts you/Plunges down."

In the same year, 1912, the poetess also made the acquaintance of the artist Franz Marc. Marc and his wife were eager to get to know the author and invited her to their home in the mountains of Bavaria, whence she, forlorn in the vast spaces of the Alpine landscape, fled to urban Munich. Franz and Maria Marc visited her there in her pension, where they found her staging mock battles on a tabletop with tin soldiers.[84] Lasker-Schüler felt an affinity with Marc's work, in which she recognized her own "respect for divine life in all creatures."[85] To Kraus she wrote in 1915: "He is such inexplicable splendor you can hardly believe that it's possible, he is the cover of the Bible . . . and what he writes from the war [Marc was at the front] dissolves again here in my hand into blood or flag or something."[86] Marc auctioned his picture "The Dream," dedicated to the Prince of Thebes, to contribute to the fund for Lasker-Schüler.[87] She dedicated to him the poem "Prayer" ("I'm searching for a city in these lands") and, after he fell in battle, memorialized him in the prose poem "Franz Marc." Letters she had written to him from 1913 to 1917, originally published in several periodicals, were collected as already mentioned in *The Malik* (1919), with, as in *My Heart* and *The Prince of Thebes*, numerous drawings by the author as well as by her artist friends, including Marc. Even more than in *My Heart*, *The Malik* records clearly that syndrome of ennui, narcissism, and alienation, along with the belief in the momentarily restorative powers of aestheticized love, which we associate with decadent writers such as Hofmannsthal and Rilke, the former of whom she despised, incidentally, for what she felt was his conscious literariness and lack of imagination. The narcissism is literal: "I have been taking opium for weeks. . . . My comrades are cowardly and miserable creatures. At night I play lover and beloved with myself; actually we're two boys. That is the chastest love-game in the world, love without goal or purpose, lovely lewdness. . . . I long now sometimes at least, if only for an evil person."[88] It is not impossible that we hear an echo of Nietzsche here, whom Lasker-Schüler credited with having created "the language in which we all write poetry."[89] She claimed to have seen Nietzsche in the decade of his madness.

Little is known about her acquaintanceship with the poet Georg Trakl, whom she met in Berlin in early 1914. Cohn assumes that their common understanding rested in part on Trakl's (presumed) incestuous relationship with his sister and Lasker-Schüler's search for a brother;[90] to Werner Kraft the poetess is reported to have expressly stated: "I always wanted a brother as a lover, then at least you know what you have, and you don't need to despise yourself."[91] Trakl would certainly have known Lasker-Schüler's "Ballad from the Mountains of the Sauerland," which appeared in *Styx* (1902) and employed the incest motif. The autistic, cheerless, and forlorn young Austrian poet might easily have recognized himself as a figure similar to the one in the poem whose "head has been turned/By a devil of a woman/His own sister."

Her sympathy with Trakl finds expression in two poems, both entitled "Georg Trakl." One is a short epitaph—Trakl, a drug addict, died from an overdose of drugs while serving as a medic during the war—and the other is a fine example of one of her fortes, the lyrical portrait sketch of a friend. Here she catches his abstracted nature and his essentially Protestant, guilt-ridden somberness. Margarete Kupper also identifies the poem "To the Knight of Gold" as being addressed to Trakl.[92]

Too numerous are Lasker-Scüler's more and less famous friends and acquaintances for them to be dealt with individually, but they include, along with her fantasy titles for them (where such exist): Franz Werfel (The Prince of Prague), Richard Dehmel—these first two she especially admired as poets—Georg Grosz, Oskar Kokoschka, Ernst Toller, Theodor Däubler, Albert Ehrenstein, Paul Zech, Peter Baum, Paul Leppin (The King of Bohemia), Hans Ehrenbaum-Degele (Tristan), Adolf Loos (The Gorilla), and Hans Adalbert von Maltzahn (The Duke of Leipzig). In letters to Kraus, Lasker-Schüler especially recognizes the attentions paid to her by Werfel, Grosz, and Däubler. (See the insightful lyrical portraits of the first two, as well as those of Richard Dehmel, the Duke of Leipzig, Peter Baum, and other artist friends.) These concise studies with their telling touches of colorful imagery are among her finest achievements.

During the years of European armed conflict and subsequent political and economic turmoil, until the death of her son Paul in 1927, no major external changes are recorded in her life. Lasker-Schüler lamented the Great War and expressly rejected it in *The Malik*, but she did not actively protest in the political realm either the war or the events of the twenties. Emotionally she sided with any suffering and opposed the destructive animosities of parties, nations, and religions, but she was not by nature equipped to deal either pragmatically or ideologically with the real world of political action.

Although her play *The Wupper* premiered in Berlin in 1919, it did nothing to revive her fortunes; the drain of lost friends went on. Her lyrical productivity slackened after the appearance of *Collected Poems* (1917), which contained many of the poems to friends. The earlier *Hebrew Ballads* (1913), a display of concentrated creative power applied to biblical figures and motifs, was poetically one of her highpoints. Several of the poems speak in the persona of Joseph, an identity that Lasker-Schüler had also adopted in *The Malik*, there too in the form of Jussuf of Egypt. From childhood, so she reports, she had cherished the figure of the biblical Joseph, perhaps, we might speculate, because of his abandonment by his brothers (reflecting her own outcast feelings) and his later role as a savior.

By the relentless calendar it was 1932 before new poetic work appeared in book form—in *Concert*. This volume contained predominantly prose essays and sketches, in some of which we come upon notable passages on the questions of love and friendship, Judaism and Christianity, and the religious impulse in general. An increased transcendence of the self is detectible in these reflections, a greater awareness of the community of human fate, a tempering of her exacerbated uniqueness. Lasker-Schüler during these years, without relinquishing her artistic pride or yielding a commensurate scorn for the bourgeoisie, increasingly loses the youthful afflatus that had borne her and admits to the bitter realization that she is ignored, that she has drifted to the periphery of the world's attention: "I no longer have any desire to be pushed into a corner, fear nobody for example, have always revenged myself and request that my humility not be confused with toadyism. There's a revolver in my hand somewhere. I respect my poetry myself but I want people to respect highly my life of hunger that I've led and perhaps also my thieves' existence."[39]

In a chill Berlin December, in 1927, her son Paul died of tuberculosis after a long illness, a loss that cast her, now fifty-eight and bereft of her closest alter ego, to the lowest level of her life. At the point of death he requested her to step behind a curtain in the room so that he might die alone—a tragic moment of implicit rejection for a woman to whom her son had seemed the very possibility of hope.[94] She never quite accepted the finality of his death; a letter written to him, prompted by a dream, is dated 1939. This incapacity surely stemmed from her strong identification with him and from her unaccepted feelings of guilt.

Although too late, perhaps, a tardy recognition finally came with the award of the Kleist prize in 1932, a satisfaction more than voided by the events of 1933 and her pell-mell flight into exile before the anti-Semitic and antiexpressionist drive of the National Socialists. Berto Perotti reports that she was knocked to the ground with an iron bar by Nazis in Berlin, and, still dazed, boarded the next train to Zurich.[95] Without means, she was picked up for vagrancy in a Swiss park by the police, and only then was the support of the Swiss literary public mobilized. Lasker-Schüler eventually managed to continue publishing in Swiss and exile periodicals, but the shock of her precipitous banishment still reverberates in the poem "Chased Away!" In 1936 a dramatic version of the mythologized story of her father, *Arthur Aronymus and His Fathers*, was given several performances in Zurich through the agency of exiled German theater people. Its well-meaning, but by that time politically naïve, intent was to reconcile Christians and Jews by good example.

Earlier, in 1934, the poetess had traveled for the first time to Jerusalem, for her a legendary Eastern land of escape like those envisioned in *Tino* and *The Prince of Thebes* but also the homeland of the Bible. Thus Jerusalem was not only a place of refuge but in her imagination a Holy Land that was symbolically interwoven with her fate, for an emotional attachment to Judaism had remained a constant all of her life.

The immediate Palestinian realities of ethnic terrorism and social need, therefore, found little expression in the chattily anecdotal and sentimentalized travel account *Land of the Hebrews* (1937), which also recalls episodes in her youth that are perhaps more psychologically significant than literally true. In 1937 she returned to Palestine a second time, and after the outbreak of World War II in 1939, her third sojourn became permanent. By then she was over seventy, although she would not admit it, was tired, ill, irritable, and driven. Impecunious because of her generosity and improvidence, she lived austerely in an unheated room and slept in a chair for want of a bed. But she had friends again, and her playful spirit had not entirely forsaken the septuagenarian; she cleaned the floor by tying oily rags around her feet and skating across it.

As ever, Lasker-Schüler fell in love, wrote poetry (indeed, some of her most beautiful love poems), held readings, and organized a lecture society. She constantly gave to others whatever she had but refused to accept casual charity for herself, believing that the artist must remain free, independent of others. Her last volume of poetry, in no way inferior to the earlier ones, came out in 1943 with the title *My Blue Piano*. A last fragmentary play, "I and I," was written during 1940 and 1941.

Else Lasker-Schüler died quietly in Jerusalem on 22 January 1945 of angina pectoris. At the end of her life she is reputed to have questioned whether the making of poems served any purpose,[96] and her last words are said to have been: "My end is coming. I can't love any more."[97] At her burial in the Jewish cemetery on the Mount of Olives, Rabbi Kurt Wilhelm read her poem beginning "I know I must soon die." During the period of Arab occupation, the building of a road removed traces of her grave, but later the tombstone was rediscovered. It contained only her name and, as she would have wanted, no record of her age in mere empirical time.

Currently, the best and most complete account of Lasker-Schüler's life is given by Sigrid Bauschinger in *Else Lasker-Schüler: Ihr Werk und ihre Zeit*, a balanced and detailed presentation to which the reader (of German) who seeks fuller access to the poetess's life and work is referred.

4.

Characterizations of Lasker-Schüler and interpretations of her work have customarily emphasized the antinomies of her nature, conflicts that are tragic for her at times, at better moments lightheartedly amusing, but in any case borne with an irreducible vitality. Her riven being can be read even in the outward occasions of her life: on the one hand, her strong, anarchic urge for independence and the boldness to break traditional taboos in dress, habit, and sexual mores; on the other, her at times infantile need—including a practical need—for the support of her patrons and friends because of her radical thriftlessness, the distraction of her mind, her refusal to calculate consequences, and the "touching helplessness" she seemed to admire in herself, about which she says: "I've noticed that even the roughest person is conquered by my fear."[98] To the very end of her life the memory of her mother, the Magna Mater in her pantheon, remained a critical emotional support.

Spiritually, the dichotomy lies between her romantic, universalized self-obsession ("I am my only immortal love") and the threatening weakness in her sense of identity.[99] Her difficulties in making true contact with other persons, her fear of disappointment, and her failure to find lasting love as she dreamed it and sought it were in constant conflict with an anxious search for identity, which had to be bolstered by fantastic masks, and with a longing for sublimely sublimated eros, which led to an insatiable appetite for (and consumption of) friends, a flight from the stifling emptiness of self. As a consequence, throughout most of her life, she could report herself simultaneously lonely and in love, ecstatic but depressed and bored.

Many critics have chosen to stress the religious longing that wells from this forlornness of the self, and indeed the authentic ardor of the later religious poems (in *My Blue Piano* and *Concert*) contrasts sharply with the more playful or mythologizing cast of the earlier ones. Kupper claims for Lasker-Schüler "a consistent concept of life that is essentially religious, with the longing for the redemption of the irredeemable world (*heillose Welt*) as its central idea."[100] Martini, too, thinks of her demand for absoluteness as a basically religious need.[101] From her youth, the images and symbols of Judaism and even of Christianity nourished her feelings and poetry, and especially toward the end of her life she addressed God humbly and personally. But in youth and the middle years, doubt and skepticism were also expressed quite frequently, and through most of her life the love songs addressed to more palpably human beings absorbed her spiritual energy.

It was rather to love that she looked, most often, for her "salvation." That love probably cannot offer it, at least not the rapturous "falling in love" that was Lasker-Schüler's mode, was likewise her tragedy; neither beloved nor friend could bear up beneath, much less requite, the intensity of her feelings and their implicit demands for the partner's unconditional surrender.

Others have detected in the poetess a potentially utopian social vision. Horst Laube writes that Lasker-Schüler was "in becoming totally conscious of herself, on the way to a radical new world of purely correct images,"[102] but even in Laube's context it is not clear what establishes the "correctness" of an image. The very notion is a contradiction, since a "correct" metaphor is a generally accepted designation and therefore no longer a metaphor. Bänsch, author of a useful if overdrawn critique of the established religious and sentimental image of the poetess, claims to be setting free through his analysis the "energy of her poetry that is directed toward changing the world," i.e., "that which is apocalyptic, the break with tradition, radicalism and the uprising against the bourgeoisie."[103] A much more negatively inclined critic, Marianne Lienau, maintains that it is precisely in this respect that Lasker-Schüler failed, that she did not transmute her iconoclasm into a "utopian model," and that furthermore her equation of "inspiration" with "revelation" implies social regression to a claim for the poet's unquestioned authority. The poetess's unintellectual, emotional boundlessness precluded the kind of self-critique that would have revealed to her her "real" and restrictively bound role in society.[104]

One can indeed cite passages in Lasker-Schüler's prose that show a consciousness of the real social world, e.g., the essay "Poor Children of Rich People,"[105] and it is beyond question that Lasker-Schüler saw herself as a member of the aesthetic elite and as an antagonist of the domesticated, monied middle class. But any such sociocritical assignment of her class position will not clarify the spirit of her poetry. If we insist upon it, her work collapses as a mere symptom of the alienated decadence of the late nineteenth-century bourgeoisie; then Laube and Bänsch are wrong and Lienau is right. But probably her work will interest us only if we find that it deals with a universal human plight, rather than presenting us with a sourcebook for sociological analysis.

Many, including myself, will prefer to read Lasker-Schüler in a more personal perspective, will see in her human fate the quandary of life's loneliness, a "longing for a second face" that, in the end, must be "content with itself," as Hans W. Cohn has put it.[106] Cohn's English-language study of the poetess's "Broken World" discriminates among the strands of her poetic work and demonstrates the various stages of a "diastole of opposites," a dialectic of "withdrawal" and "outgoing."[107] The backward movement proceeds in the stages: disappointment and resentment; despair and isolation; escape into fantasy (childhood, lost paradise, mother, play, masks); and finally preoccupation with death (death wishes, death-in-life, death as transition, and conquest of death.) The forward or outgoing movement rises from the longing for contact, through the erotic encounter (sexual need, wish for union) to the search for God (Judaism, the Bible, Jewish mysticism, changing images of God, the figure of Christ, Jerusalem.) This dialectic scheme outlines a reasonably complete catalog of motifs and themes in a useful perspective.[108]

Like any abstract, however, it cannot capture the breathing creatures of poetry—here, the strong and vivid moments of an impulsive woman seeking devotion, or the chill vastation of her abandonment, whether abandoned through death or the faithlessness of others or by her own unconscious instigation. For the receptive reader, I think, Lasker-Schüler's brief and simple poems will still deliver her urgent telegrams of joy and fear, though at the time of their dispatching they may not always have evoked the desired response from their addressees.

5.

The present volume contains translations of poems collected in the Kösel-Verlag edition: *Else Lasker-Schüler: Gedichte 1902–1943*. Lasker-Schüler or her publishers often included previously published poetry in later, differently titled volumes, sometimes in a slightly altered version, so that occurrence in a given volume does not always indicate the time of original appearance. Here the poems are usually in their original context (as found in the Kösel edition) save for a few second versions that have been preferred to the first, some poems that first appeared in prose works, and several poems presented here among the thematically unified *Hebrew Ballads* (1913) although their first occurrence was earlier.

As is usually the case with translations, the poems selected are mainly those that yielded adequately to my own efforts at translation and, in the original, are successful as a whole or include some interesting passage; but there are some that are simply meant to add to the variety of representation or to illustrate a remark in the Introduction. Needless to say, not all of those in the last two categories belong to the irreducible stock of timeless German lyrics and, of course, other critics might wish to include, or exclude, other poems.

At times, fully rhymed originals have been rendered in only partial rhyme or with a somewhat different scheme; comparison with the facing German text will make this clear. A number of good poems I have not yet been able to translate with sufficient fidelity to the original form, and these are unfortunately absent; they are often the longer poems with more complicated stanza schemes. Since the free-verse poems translate most readily, they are overrepresented, but in my opinion it is often just these in which Lasker-Schüler's entrancing rhythm and cameo images most excel. Somewhat less than half of the total Kösel-Verlag collection is offered here.

Though the basic themes of Lasker-Schüler's art persist through all of her books, lines of thematic and formal development do exist; for ease of comparison the poems are separated by volume in the table of Contents. Her first-born (*Styx*, 1902) contains, if we may believe the poetess, some poems that had been written in her adolescent years, from the age of fifteen to seventeen. In this volume she had not yet developed her most characteristic metrical style—the two- and three-line, free-verse strophes—but her rhymed forms are often handled freely in terms of meter and stanzaic structure. The use of extravagant, grotesque, intensifying metaphor is already her own. The main themes—love, dejection, religious feeling, her child—are all convoked, but verses astir with a candid erotic passion are more prominent than in her settled years, and, on the whole, the taste of the times shows through. But despite its reflection of literary fashion, the volume contains some fine lyrics.

Echoes of neoromanticism, decadence, and art nouveau can be heard in the titles: "Jealousy," "Instinct," "My Blush," "Nervus Erotis," "Vagabonds," "Old Spring," "Orgy," "Fever," "Eros," "Sensual Ecstasy"; or, in the fashion of romantic demonism: "Damnation," "Chaos," "Weltschmerz," "The Fallen Angel," "Suicide," "Guilt," "Unhappy Hate," "After-Pain," "Revenge," "The Fear Deep in My Blood."

The desire for love is there, and for union, both sexual and spiritual. Complete union is the goal, a spiritual state that rejects real circumstances and exists at a perpetually high pitch. It cannot, like simple friendship, be induced or cultivated; it either takes place between two people or it does not. Lasker-Schüler deprecates mere "love," which is bourgeois, compared with her own overpowering "falling in love" (*verliebt sein*), a faculty in which she knows that few can match her, for, in the same breath she goes on to say, "Or somebody must have loved me. Did you love me, Herwarth? Who loved me?"[109]

She herself did not hesitate to give the answer: she herself. For the love that remained true after the disappointment of unresponsive and unfaithful lovers was narcissistic; "I am my only immortal love," she said at one time, with obvious pleasure in her aphorism, however painful the fact.[110] A friend, Grete Fischer, opines, "She was in love with love. I hardly believe that she was in love with the men about whom she speaks with such enthusiasm."[111] The poetess confided to Karl Kraus, "I know so many people I write a love poem for six people together"; and "The only important thing is how I give expression to the models. I have nothing further to do with them"; and "I only need people to furnish my stars."[112] She wrote to Walden, "I never perceived people other than as a frame in which I put myself."[113]

But it would be a mistake to press this psychological catechizing to an extreme. Unquestionably she had known real love—for Peter Hille, Gottfried Benn, Johannes Holzmann, her son, her mother. And despite the professional cynicism of the artist in her *bons mots* to Karl Kraus, her friends and Lasker-Schüler herself record repeated infatuations on her part until advanced age; the beautiful "A Love Song" appeared in her last book. Shades of Goethe! (And was Goethe always "really" in love?)

She may have been well aware that these fleeting enchantments were a game, but it was *her* vital game, the talent, along with her gift for language, that gave meaning to her life as a homeless transient. Love was for her a source of vitality and a resurrection of the spirit, the counteractive to hate and violence, as we read in the poem "Autumn," where her memories of National Socialist torchlight parades may also be invoked: "Eternal life to *him* who can say much of love./ A being of *love* will rise most certainly!/Hate boxes in! High though the torch may flare above."

It is less clear what we are to think of Lasker-Schüler's personal erotic propensities. There are some torridly beautiful verses in *Styx*, for example in "Sensual Ecstasy" or in these lines from "Fortissimo": "And our desire came breaking loose/And hunted us in blood-storm swells:/We sank into the Smyrna moss/Gone wild and screaming like gazelles." The arsenal of images in the early poems is bristling with fires, conflagrations, glowings, pourings, sinkings, plungings. Curiously enough, we have no way of verifying to what extent these poetic visions record actual desires or erotic adventures. Other than her possible but puzzling affair with the father of her child, the nebulous Alcibiades de Rouan, it is difficult to pin down a specifically sexual encounter, although it is sometimes assumed her relationship with Benn was such. To be sure, Kurt Hiller accused her of seducing young poets to win their loyalty "in a base way"; but this unchivalrous charge aroused her intense and apparently honest indignation.[114] Here, offended honor was involved, but, in addition, a kind of aesthetic prudishness can be detected in what she allegedly said to Sigismund von Radecki: "The physical act by which a human being is created is something so impossible that it is only justified when two people, because of their love, simply can't do otherwise."[115] Nevertheless, in her own prose writings, more reliable than Radecki's report, what we find is a balanced view of spiritual and physical love, not at all Victorian or Wilhelminian: "I am thence at least capable of understanding man's body, which God created after his primordial image. And I wonder why one should despise this image, the flesh, the covering of the soul, especially since we enjoy the foliage of the forest, luxuriantly dense, and of each individual tree; why not the beauty of the bodily temple, which preserves in itself a treasure, the most holy, the soul."[116] The imagery here is itself probably sexual. The body, i.e., sexuality, was for her in her later essayistic writings a pathway to and for the soul. Lasker-Schüler sees even the prostitute's profession as just a pretext; even she is only looking for a residue of paradise: "Love is always a psychic possession, sexuality its chalice. To reject sexuality thus would mean not to respect the body that hosts the soul. This often occurs erroneously. But I think sexuality is to be condemned which isn't seeking love's paradise. I praise the Don Juan, who, through all the hearts, is only seeking the paradisical one. Naturally there is a love, prepared in the love-light of God's East, which needs no chalice."[117]

Cohn maintains that this latter, unchaliced love is given pride of place by Lasker-Schüler.[118] This does not necessarily emerge from the passage or the context, although it is true that platonic relationships such as hers to Johannes Holzmann ("Senna Hoy") were important occasions of her life, almost parareligious experiences. Yet the above passage was written from the viewpoint of a woman in later years and need not express the attitude of the author of the *Styx*. Actually, only the poems themselves tell us about the force of eros in Lasker-Schüler's youth, and if we believe them—even discounting a bit of literary pose—it was a drive of which she was much aware, whether or not (very likely not) it was promiscuously indulged. Cohn himself points out the candor and mature psychological self-observation of poems like "Instinct," where "the expression of sexual need does not betray any feeling of guilt."[119]

Both specific and oblique sexual imagery abounds in the poetry. In contrast to the body-soul harmony promulgated in her later prose writings, the sexual drive may be depicted as an uncontrollable force or attack to which she submits will-lessly ("Instinct"), or as a torture ("Instinct") or narcotic ("Sensual Ecstasy"), while in another mood it is felt as a joyful, inseparable union of rushing cataracts ("Viva!") or the wild rapture of gazelles ("Fortissimo"). In "Knowledge," she celebrates the "primal cry, the song of Eve," whose "longing was the snake"; and in "Flight of Love" (from *The Seventh Day*, her second book of lyrics) a lover "leaped with me on the winds,/Godwards, until our breath gave way." The whole spectrum of the sex drive's sometimes alien, sometimes exultant, but always overmastering force is clearly projected from: "Let's whet our lusts in hellish heats" ("Vagabonds") to "Now like two children let us play" ("Spring").

Yet there are also indications of resentment at the power of this instinctive drive. In "Karma" the speaker mutters morosely, "In a night of stars all blazing free/I killed the man who was next to me"; and in "His Blood," the tormented blood (read "natural instinct") of the lover would "really prefer to pluck my joy's/Last rose in Maytime/ And throw it in the gutter slime." In the poem "My Drama" the poetess seems to resent being "lured" and thinks her beloved is, if the truth were told, "afraid" of her; she is miserable, longs for her loneliness and has learned "hate for my body, my heart's blood and him." In the uncharacteristically Gothic "Ballad from the Mountains of the Sauerland," it is the woman figure who exercises a demonic domination destructive to the man, and in "Elegy," a love "which had died young" drives her "exhausted into Satan's arms."

It has frequently been noted that there was a distinct masculine component in Lasker-Schüler's nature.[120] She wore short hair and sometimes pants, before these became customary feminine attributes. Her mythical masks (in the prose) were often male—the Prince of Thebes, Jussuf of Egypt—although in her poems she normally speaks in her own woman's voice. Perhaps close identification with father, brother, son, and platonic lovers reinforced this tendency, though certainly her mother was a primary guiding figure in her life. However, the poems themselves only infrequently hint at any homoerotic tendencies, e.g., in "Old Spring." More often the relation of two ostensible males ("Pharaoh and Joseph" or "David and Jonathan") is really more like that of male and female, with the poetess speaking from the female point of view. Most of the imagery presupposes a feminine self-conception of freely chosen devotedness, along with the unquestioned acceptance of an emotionally strong sexual role, both experienced within the limits of an absolute personal independence. In this respect, despite some turn-of-the-century arabesques of sentiment and literary allusion, she seems to me quite modern in her realization of an autonomous femininity, with all the open potentials for gratification and disaster that any extreme autonomy of character imports.

6.

The Seventh Day (1905), the next volume of lyrics, was dedicated to her mother as *Styx* had been to both "dear parents." It was published by a different house, as indeed almost each of her books was; she was convinced of the exploitative intent of her successive publishers and compared their enterprises to the "bordellos of soul-merchants."[121] This book, about half the size of the previous one, contains several poems considerably longer than preceding efforts ("Knowledge," "My Quiet Song")—a departure that was soon abandoned. Here also appeared some early unrhymed triadic stanzas ("Dove That Swims in Its Own Blood," "My Love Song") and the unrhymed two-line stanzas ("My Quiet Song") that proved to be Lasker-Schüler's most unique and fruitful formal innovations, later perfected into the hymnic earmark of her work. (Two brief rhymed two-liners, "Weltschmerz" and "Karma," had been published in *Styx*.)

Thematically, the *Seventh Day* is familiar, although several humorous poems open new territory ("School Days," "Grotesque"), but the best examples of her irony and grotesque humor are naturally in the prose. "The End of the World," adopting a favorite motif of the expressionists, implies the death of God, while other poems are preoccupied with human mortality, her fear of which was undoubtedly sharpened by perceiving the transitoriness of her own feelings. The poet is obviously well on the way to her personal imaginative and metric style, though literary echoes still can be heard—for example, of Stefan George in "Fighters" ("Streiter," not included here.) The best attempts are in the new rhymeless forms.

7.

In *My Miracles* (1911) we witness the ripening mastery of poems written in two- or three-line strophes or in a mixture of various verse-group lengths. Among these stand the first of the biblical poems, such as the fine "Pharaoh and Joseph," as well as her perhaps most famous lyric, "An Old Tibetan Rug."

This signatory style of Lasker-Schüler has often been compared to the metric of paralleled members (*parallelismus membrorum*) employed by Hebrew poetry, as in the *Psalms*, but parallelism in the sense of repeated syntactical structures or of the pairing of synonymous or substantively related (or contrasted) images is not present. Lasker-Schüler claimed to have read frequently in the Bible, but her familiarity with it has been questioned.[122] Nevertheless, in her verses as in biblical poetry we experience a comparable series of brief paratactic statements, heavy with imagery but without metrical regularity.

It may be significant, regarding the question of influence, that the poetess once claimed in her half-serious, half-ironic way that her poems were written in Hebrew.[123] Because of this affinity her characteristic form has been called by Martini "mythically old and at the same time very modern. . . . Modernity was ready for the forms of the archaic,"[124] an idea recalling Thomas Mann's theory of modern art in *Doctor Faustus* as an intellectualized reversion to primitive forms. But in Lasker-Schüler's poetry there is no trace of the "bloodless intellectuality" allied with "bloody barbarism" that is found in Adrian Leverkühn's music. Her poems give voice to the "soul" that Leverkühn lacked.

These short strophes in free verse are by no means without rhythmic principles, but they are mainly principles of proportion. There are, for example, usually limits to the number of emphatic stresses grouped in a strophe; in "Pharaoh and Joseph," in the German original, this number varies from five to nine. Strophes may show the same number of emphases in each verse or may contain both longer and shorter lines, variations in this point enlivening the rhythm. Most frequently, syntax and strophe proceed in congruence—each verse group comprises a single sentence; sometimes, however, the syntax is allowed to enjamb. Verse-end pauses may coincide with any phrasal juncture but will not intervene within a prepositional or noun phrase. More than in regular metrical poetry there is a strong interaction between breath grouping and the endings of verse and stanza. A rhythmic factor hardly to be overestimated in its importance is the overlapping enchainment of inner assonance, which does so much to provide continuity to the rhythmic flow. In this, Lasker-Schüler is a master. A grasp of the dynamic relationship of repeated sounds is a vital compositional skill in the euphony of free verse, and we have been told that even as a child Lasker-Schüler was sensitive to the disharmony of off-rhymes (though they litter her poems and were thus probably consciously accepted as a means of expressive freedom).

The phenomenological correlative of these devices, in concord, has been described as "dreamspun music,"[125] "magical monotony,"[126] or a "proclamatory tone" such as that in Old Testament poetry.[127] At its best, it mildly hypnotizes and creates the same hyperaesthesia as meter, but more than regular meter it alerts the listener to the palpable objective silence that the poet's words must dominate. The images are strung in luminous isolation, each suspended in a moment of unique tension, each subject to time's immediate decay. Psychologically, the representations proceed more as in memory or in dream than as in conscious reflection or in direct reality. Lasker-Schüler has in this way realized the necessary aesthetic distance from her emotions, which tend to be unrestrained or sentimentalized. Ceremonious attention, even solemnity, reins the affections; a reposeful measuredness is insinuated by the strophic rhythm.

This dream-speech can, of course, also lapse into mere routine, a mechanical mannerism,[128] but that is true in the same degree of regular metrical poetry; we are simply more attuned to, and thus unaware of, the strictures of the latter. One specific source of potential monotony in this particular form, however, is the lack of interaction between a rhythmic norm and the norm's incomplete realization in concrete language. Since there is no fixed standard, we lose the sense of variety. This is a debility in all free verse, but particularly in Lasker-Schüler's short verses and sentences (as opposed to long rhapsodic lines of free verse), which arouse an expectation of proportional rhythmic form but lack a firm norm that could underline moments of expressive change. At times they may fail to escape repetitiveness and may become a "flowing into boundlessness,"[129] which never reaches the intended end of movement in fulfilled repose.[130] Actually, from the viewpoint of both logic and thematic development, Lasker-Schüler has occasional trouble in gathering her poems to an effective conclusion, a weakness consequent in part on her effusive, imagistic style.

A traditional topos employed by tone-deaf critics is the supposedly crushing announcement that free verse sounds no different than prose, a charge supported by typographical resetting of the poem in question in a prose format. Dieter Bänsch does just this with Lasker-Schüler, and *mirabile dictu*—at the magic swish of a scholar's pointer-wand—the poem indeed then sounds like prose.[131] But, naturally, one has destroyed the whole structure of rhythm in the process and should not be proud of the results. The reverse transformation is just as astonishing (if not more so); real prose reset in short lines that introduce rhythmic proportions and recurrent pauses, thus focusing attention on the sounds themselves, will lead a reader to assume the heightened ethos of poetic performance.

We have every reason to believe that the finely tuned rhythm we hear in these poems was the music heard by Lasker-Schüler herself. In her recitations she was credited with a "masterful" delivery, carried by a "dark, melodic, expressive voice,"[132] however odd her other sound effects (bells, flutes) and her exorbitant garb may have appeared. Her conscious theory concerning the relationship between breathing and poetry[133] led her to report that she felt "bodily injury from a vowel or consonant that causes undefined disturbances in measure or hearing" (meter or sound harmony is what she probably meant.)[134] Not infrequently her *regular* metrical forms show deviations from their given schemes. One cannot be sure that she consciously scanned her verses (I rather imagine she would have thought that pedantry), but it is precisely in the nature of free verse that one dare spurn such Philistine niceties as scansion, and the poet's inner rhythm can hold sway.

8.

In *My Miracles* we first take note of recurring motifs that acquire symbolic value. These verbal counters seem to be extremely important for the poetess, even if in their later persistence they at times begin to ring hollow.

Foremost among these hieroglyphs is certainly the "star." Even visually, Lasker-Schüler was fascinated by the star as conventionally drawn; her sketches frequently imprint it on the cheek or brow of human faces, on buildings, even show it, as Philistines might expect, in the sky. Such drawings come to mind then when we read: "I am a star/In the blue cloud of your face" (from "But Your Brows Are a Storm"), where the image also bears a symbolic meaning. Her letters, too, are full of pictorial doodlings and ideographs, including frequent stars.

But the meaning of "star" as a metaphor is somewhat elusive. The poem "Say It Softly" begins "You took for yourself all the stars/ Above my heart," and in "Reconciliation" we are informed, "There will be a giant star fall in my womb," and in "Evening" (not included here), "A weeping angel carves the inscription/On the pillar of my body in stars." The natural and conventional symbolism of stars includes the semantic features: brilliance, distance, fateful significance, order, everlastingness. Such meanings may often be applied in Lasker-Schüler's poems; the "star" there may suggest a high, incandescent moment of feeling, or something or someone of unchanging brilliance, a lodestar inaccessible to the lower creatures of the earth. Cohn sees the image simply as a symbol of transcendence,[135] which perhaps lacks in precision because it ignores the suggestions of radiance and significance. For Muschg the star is the "absolutely miraculous, the grace of love"; to bear it on one's face is a sign of the elect.[136] In Georges Schlocker's view the star becomes a token of the "miraculous worlds" to which the poetess aspires[137] out of her constitutional ennui.

In a little noted essay titled "Astrology," in the volume *Visions* (*Gesichte*), Lasker-Schüler contrasts the original chaos in the self, which is palpable and the source of suffering, with the "star system" in the same self, which is untouchable and regulatory: "I speak of your most invisible, of your highest part, which you cannot grasp, like the stars above you."[138] The descent of God's son to earth, for example, is a "transformation from star into chaos." (Lasker-Schüler speaks figuratively here to express God's entry into the earthly being of Jesus.)[139]

An "undisturbed astral course" is what determines the greatness of human figures, like St. Peter Hille,[140] whereas human ills stem from the collision of "stars strayed from their paths."[141] One dies of "burst stars or the chilling of your sun or from darkness."[142] In this "astrological" context, we can understand the stars as the vital determinant forces of each human fate, whose harmonious constellation and unabating energy light up the chaos of the unconscious life and whose clear radiance attracts other souls charismatically. A star as a person is a kind of spiritual guardian: "O she was a staress—/Strewed shimmering light around her" ("Alice Trübner"); or "All of my dreams hang from your gold;/I have chosen you among all stars" ("Secretly at Night"). Lasker-Schüler was not versed in conventional symbolism, but it is interesting to note in conjunction with the "Astrology" essay that J. E. Cirlot's *Dictionary of Symbols*, based on a multicultural survey, finds that the star "stands for the forces of the spirit struggling against the forces of darkness," a meaning that, Cirlot claims, appears worldwide in emblematic art.[143]

The poetess's astral views help to explain such otherwise abstruse verses as: "See my colors/Black and star" ("To Giselheer the Heathen"), where black represents material chaos and the curious adjective "star" suggests the transcendent light, both of which poles she recognizes in herself and others. In "Reconciliation," with its initial line "There will be a giant star fall in my womb," she expects a miraculous regenerative force to accompany her reconciliation with the person addressed; life will be renewed; "Whenever we embrace we do not die." The ambiguity of the word *Schoß* in the original of this poem, meaning either "lap" or "womb," imports a subliminally erotic image that also suggests the renewal of life through procreation. The common interpretation of this poem sees it as referring primarily to the Day of Atonement. This view is supported in the text by the prayer in a harp-shaped alphabet, i.e., Hebrew, by the overflow of God, and by the word "Versöhnung," which in German also occurs in the translation of Yom Kippur. This theory, however, overlooks the obviously given situation that a lover is addressing her beloved and the fact that the word "versöhnen" in the original appears as a reflexive ("Wir wollen uns versöhnen die Nacht"), almost certainly indicating a personal reconciliation rather than a ritual of atonement.

A closely related symbol is the color *blue*, which Cohn terms the "color of the spirit" or of "spiritual peace."[144] Blue, Schlocker contends, is the "covering of the divine," a cue that opens vast "spiritual spaces" for Lasker-Schüler.[145] Blue is in fact often associated with an immaterial realm of purity by natural symbolism; Cirlot lists thinking, truth, equilibrium, religious feeling, heaven, devotion, and innocence as correlatives of blue in various cultures.[146] In "Say It Softly" the blueness of the eyes of her lover has been stolen from an archangel, and in "I Am Sad" the lover appears "Blue from [caused by] Paradise," suggesting heavenliness, calm, integrity, and innocence. The same qualities make sense of her claim in "Prayer": "I brought love to the world, and light—/So every heart can blossom forth in blue."

Gold, say Muschg and Cohn, has an erotic connotation for the poetess;[147] they have in mind, perhaps, lines such as "And like the moon of gold—your body" in "From Afar," a poem not included here. For Guder it implies nobility or is mere decoration.[148] In Cirlot's broader cultural view it is the color of superiority and glory, correspondent to the sun.[149] It is indeed true in Lasker-Schüler's work that *gold* most commonly appears in the physical description of people, often to glorify the color of skin or hair, or generally to exalt the feature described. Erotic overtones are perhaps intended in "A Love Song": "A night of gold;/Stars made of night . . . /Nobody sees us"; but these are less likely in a metaphor such as "Golden icons/Are your eyes," in the poem "When I Met Tristan," also not included here.

Other motifs, such as the *angel, wing, flower, sea, night, mother,* and *heart,* would reward an effort at more exact definition, but they often adhere to the natural, conventional, or figurative implications of the words. Nevertheless, reference to Lasker-Schüler's prose is sometimes helpful. When she writes in *Concert,* in the essay "Friendship and Love," that unrequited love is a case of the wings of love's angel being broken, we immediately recall the first stanza of "Prayer":

> I'm searching for a city in these lands
> Before whose gate a mighty angel stands;
> For, broken at the shoulder blade,
> I bear his wings' gigantic spans,
> And on my brow his star as seal is laid.

The dejected and forlorn poetess searches for the angel of love, love that is not returned but whose broken wing (the power of love's flight) she possesses and whose star (symbol of a guiding light) is imprinted on her brow—as in the sketches she never tired of drawing.

9.

Hebrew Ballads (1913) enjoys a greater degree of thematic unity than any of its predecessors. Its topics are all religious, mainly profiles of biblical figures or episodes, hardly ballads at all, but reinterpretations or original legends with a powerful immediacy of their own. This biblical involvement presages, but does not as yet fulfill, the later turn to a more personal religious lyricism. In this volume—not constricted by fidelity to the letter of the Testament—she conjures up her own visions of Abraham, Jacob, Joseph, and others, setting them in a poetic world that, as Bänsch correctly notes, is as characteristic of the turn-of-the-century scene as it is of early Hebraic history.[150] The portrait of "Jacob," for example, bears little resemblance to its subject, but its titanism and narcissistic smile of defeat (or victory) would seem quite in order for a hero of the decadence.

These historical motifs produce an effect of objectivity, because the poems, even when spoken in the first person, are constrained in part by the factual model and hence mask to some extent the poet's subjectivity. This quality makes the *Hebrew Ballads*, for Hans Cohn, "the most evenly excellent of all her collections,"[151] and Fritz Martini affirms that with this book she became the greatest poet of Jewish faith writing in German in the twentieth century.[152]

From the aesthetic point of view, these poems are indeed more consistently harmonious structures than those of the earlier creative periods. Compared with Rilke's biblical poetry, Bänsch states, they may seem "more Old Testament-like, more inelegant, more naïve." "Like in an edifying book for children," Bänsch remarks, "little stories are unfolded."[153] But there are moments of terse drama in Lasker-Schüler's language, the repertoire of images is refreshed, and a chiseled, archaic quality is achieved in poems like "Abraham and Isaac" or "Moses and Joshua," which is more robust than Rilke's suave rhythms and subtle perceptions.

Lasker-Schüler's relationship to Judaism was personally and culturally deep but not theologically exclusive. She called herself a "most fervent Hebrew"[154] and was, as Cohn says, "profoundly conscious of being a Jew"[155]—even as a child she had been exposed to anti-Semitism—but her religious piety toward life encompassed everyone of comparable good faith, be it a Catholic Hille or a Protestant-born Benn. The Bible strongly influenced her themes and style; certain Judaic conceptions, such as paradise and the fall, she grasped in terms of her loss of childhood's security, and Eve became a symbol of her womanhood as did Jerusalem of the final homeland. She knew a bit about Jewish mysticism; what she was familiar with in the Jewish literary tradition is unclear.[156] Yet all of these circumstances, as significant as they are, do not add up to a doctrinal faith but rather more to a tradition of religious culture. She identified with the Jewish people (see "My People") but actually more, according to Sigismund von Radecki, with the "wild, Maccabean Jews."[157] In her own words, "It's fine to be a Jew . . . if one has remained true to it, grown part of it, not misled by any external triviality, but washed by the Jordan. Who can tear me away from the old skeleton of Jehovah, the unshakable rock."[158]

Yet she did not countenance the fractioning of religion by a sectarian spirit. Lack of theological rigor is evident in her ambiguous attitude toward the figure of Jesus. She was not beyond calling him the Messiah or God's son,[159] and she could even say, perhaps in a mood to flabbergast the middle classes, that "the Jew who rejects the Heavenly One [Jesus] proves that he is a bourgeois."[160] She wrote a poem to Mary and often refers to the Nazarene, but it was as human figures that she was devoted to them, as part of her heritage of Jewish religious paragons like the characters of the Old Testament, "the people of the primordial stories who laid the roots of mankind."[161] Her love for Jesus and his mission, for his apostles, and for early Christianity extends only through the time of the early Christians' persecution.[162] In later years she wrote, "Today I am sympathetic only to individual persons, whatever their religion may be."[163] Ernst Ginsberg claims that in the early thirties Lasker-Schüler was on the point of converting to Catholicism,[164] but, even should that be the case (and it is not hinted at elsewhere), one should not assume it would have basically changed her eclectic religious views or her loyalty to her mythical Joseph, to "My People" or to Jerusalem. For her there was only "one faith, one God, one creation, one heaven."[165] In exile in the real Jerusalem of strife and tension, she hoped in vain to find a "reconciliation" realized and in the end, Cohn notes, found her refuge to be spiritually dead,[166] a sentiment underlying the poem "Jerusalem." But not even that could mar her spirit's mythical city.

10.

No genre of the lyric is so uniquely Lasker-Schüler's as the pointillistic portraits of her beloved ones and friends, those of the former largely hymnic, those of the latter sometimes chatty and informal. Both come to the fore in the *Collected Poems* (1917), which adds to the reprinted earlier works those new series of poems dedicated severally to Senna Hoy, Hans Ehrenbaum-Degele, Gottfried Benn, Hans Adalbert von Maltzahn, and to "My Beautiful Mother." In the first four series are gathered some of her finest love poems in two- and three-line stanzas, works that are usually eulogistic but containing a few, particularly among those to Benn, that express the dejection of disappointed love and reproach the beloved, usually mildly. The last two series unite sketches of her numerous friends with poems to her sister and child, some of them drawn from earlier books. In "My Beautiful Mother" rhyme schemes reappear, and love poetry is absent. The portraits of friends in the Maltzahn group share the situational objectivity of the *Hebrew Ballads* and, like them, expand the previous range of motifs and feelings, thus breaking the spell of a style that tended increasingly toward automatism. These works vividly recreate for us the atmosphere of the poetess's activities and companionship in Berlin during the most youthfully vigorous and outgoing years of her life, and they add a certain ballast of social reality to the solitary, burning elevations in which the poetess confronts her beloved. Whether or not these vignettes of admiring friendship truthfully reproduce their subjects, they are at least poetic artifacts in their own right, sharply limned mosaics in bright pinpointed colors.

11.

The late poems of Else Lasker-Schüler, harvest of the sorrows of penurious years and endless loneliness, of her son's death and the terror of her flight and exile, spread a mood of resignation sometimes succumbing to hopelessness; yet they also speak the language of an increasingly humble personal piety in some of her best religious lyrics such as "God Hear . . ." in *Concert* (1932), "Prayer" in *My Blue Piano* (1943), the movingly dignified elegy to her dead son ("To My Child"), and her apotheosis of love in "Autumn." The poetess returns to a contemplation of her own experience within now accepted limits of reality and in a less mannered style. The love poems, no longer in the majority, are less imperative, more modest, more touching in their honest respect for the otherness of the beloved.

Lasker-Schüler's relationship to God began in childish fantasy and ended in childlike faith. The God of her earlier poems may at one moment be a playful young father, wagging a finger with forced jollity at an even younger rascal of a poet ("In the Beginning"), while only shortly later it appears that God has precipitately aged and died ("End of the World") or at least absconded. "God, where are you?" she asks in "To God" (not included here). Bänsch quips that she treats God as one more poetic figure among others, almost as a painted decoration.[167] But there is also a real and lasting skepticism in her soul. We have previously quoted her letter to Karl Kraus in 1914, when she was already forty-five years of age: "Waves are always beating on my heart; I always have to go over God's grave; I almost believe he's dead and the Bible is his tombstone. For human feelings it can only seem like willfulness—if he lives and has turned away."[168] True to decadent rhetoric, Satan plays in the early poems a more reliably present role than God ("Damnation," "Elegy").

Her feelings are marked by a vacillation between skepticism and a picture-book image of God the Father, between fear of his disappearance and the devotion of the mystical bride. She admits, "It is so easy to assert that there is no God"[169] but confesses too, "I was always busy digging, not for gold but for God. I didn't dig for the eternal out of bold arrogance but from religious adventure-lust."[170] The tone of her late poems is caught in an essay entitled "My Devotion," from *Concert*: "I rely on God, because how often I have put my pain and joy into his hands."[171] At this point she has apparently overcome the doubt that is prompted by the perennial problem of theodicy: how it is that God's omnipotence can tolerate evil, in particular the suffering of her soul, which longs to be devout? The world of the suffering body is here seen as an illusion, a mere "crystallization of the soul's homeward longing for protection in God the Father's hands,"[172] and it is thus of lesser reality. Perhaps she should have said, "God the Mother," because God's protectiveness toward the world is seen as the relation of mother and child.[173] In any event, in her last poems a child's trustful submission to the parent's will is the experiential ground of her faith. God has become an imperative and not just a poetic image with which to convey charming beliefs or resentful desolations.

The propensity toward faith was a lifelong implication of her divided character: her constitutional commingling of sharp anxiety and dulled feeling, her sense of being a lonely outcast in society and yet suffocated by its grip, this latter an impression that in several respects—culminating in her persecution and forced exile—was only too close to the truth. God's was then the only reassuring love that would never reject or disappoint.

Her letters, real and fictional, repeatedly report that she is alone,[174] even though she knows nice people,[175] even in the Café of the West.[176] She cannot find a bridge to anyone's soul.[177] "Nobody can get to me, I can't get to anybody."[178] She loves no one,[179] and no one loves her.[180] Life is purposeless; one takes refuge in one's self: "We're only on the way; life is just a way, has no arrival, because it isn't coming from anywhere. Where should one go anyway? Take refuge in yourself! That's why people are so poor, their hearts are asylums; they feel themselves secure in their sociable homesteads."[181] She is driven to "flee mewards," in her "Flight from the World."

"I could never be compared with other people," she opined in a letter to Herwarth Walden,[182] and she thought of herself as an Indian, a Robinson Crusoe, a Theban prince, Joseph the Egyptian, anybody but a mere Frau Else Lasker-Schüler, put down like a million others with their inexorable birth dates in a file in an archive in a swarming city somewhere on the Brandenburger flats. Her fantasy worlds were theatrically cozy homesteads envisioned by a homeless wanderer, who also, repeatedly and to great effect, burned bridges she had not yet built across the human stream.

But the stage behind these fantastic props stood empty again as soon as the poetess's audience had left. She was bored, benumbed, but apprehensive and afraid of death:

> I cannot find myself again
> In this dead abandonment!
> It's as if: I lie world-far from me
> Among gray night of old anxiety.
> ["Chaos"]

Urangst, "old anxiety," is for Cohn a key word, expressing the mood of her "rootlessness and isolation."[183] It is the pathos of self-abandonment and helplessness, draining away the essential elán of life. In "Spring Sorrow" this "repose of death" is to be revivified by an infusion of her lover's warming "spring-like blood," for probably, as in "Revenge" (not included here), "Death spent the night in my soul/And ate my springtimes." This ebbing of vitality is the victory of death's forces ("The Fear Deep in My Blood"), which, on more manic occasion ("Youth"), is roundly defied: "Why *me* in the City of the Dead,/Me, whose rejoicing's just begun." Symptomatically, a condition of listless dread and paralysis of feeling gives way to a spell of rebelliousness: "And my soul lies there like a pale, wide plain/And hears life grinding in the mill,/Dissolving in a heavy chill,/And gathering hot for battle once again" (in "Fighters," not included here.) With the passing of youth, however, the resistance of sheer animal vitality had to give way to courage or to faith.

In the prose works Lasker-Schüler's depressive ennui is plainly described. She is "restless with fearful boredom."[184] She is tired of life and wants to die adventuresomely: 'I'm fed up with everything, even the leaves on the trees. Always green and always green. If only I'd meet some magical people, I mean some who had grand wishes, but they are all serious, only I am in earnest. I'm so lonely—whoever looks at me for a long time will fall into a dark—heaven."[185] "I'm through; I hate to wake up in the morning because I hate the world; I don't want to sleep because I dream of the world."[186] She clearly recognizes that this spiritual vastation is the obverse of her spiritual freedom: "I no longer have anything to hold on to. . . . I never made a system for myself like smart women do, never fortified a world-view like still smarter men, I haven't built myself an ark. I am unattached."[187] Because she was unattached personally (especially after the death of Paul) and to an extent also socially (especially in exile), and because she served no ideology other than her art and found it to be unrecognized even in her Promised Land, she in the end turned back to her happier beginning and saw the power of love in herself not as hers to be requited—as such it had overpowered both others and herself—but as a divine presence: "Holy love which you blindly trampled/Is God's image." ("I Lie Somewhere by the Side of the Road," not included here.) Love is the completed bridge between herself and God, to whom she could now proffer her soul with the modesty of a woman returning a lost possession to its rightful owner: "Oh God, though it of fault be full—/Take it quietly in your hand. . . . /That, in you, it may gleam—and end" ("Prayer").

12.

The potency of love is the immanence of God. This conviction becomes not only a religious principle but an aesthetic one as well, in the form: creativity is divine inspiration, hence a revelation, a belief that leads Bänsch to speak of Lasker-Schüler's "undaunted romantic definition of art and the founding of religion" as one and the same.[188] She says, "I even assert that the artist who has overcome ambition is concerned only with the Nirvana of inspiration, drifting off into sleep, the streaming away of the heart, making room for God."[189] A true work of art proceeds from a state of enthusiasm (*Schwärmerei*; the English word literally means to have God in oneself);[190] and it is this state of the soul that is to be sought, not the poet's probably faulty record of the experience: "It is not the poem that is important, but the poetic state in which one creates it."[191] Put thus, it sounds quite like the expressionist poetics, which extols the poet's intensity, ethical or aesthetic, rather than the technical perfection of his actual poems. The poetic state transcends the inadequacies of life as it sadly is; it is a resurrection: "I die from life and catch my breath again in images."[192] So, despite her poverty, her writing made her rich: "I've been composing poetry now for two days and two nights; I'm actually a person who has many palaces. I can enter my poetdom, as wide as a thousand mornings and nights—and I cannot lose it, and the very fact that one must pay his taxes with his blood—that is possession."[193]

We might be led to think that for Lasker-Schüler the poet's office is austerely sacerdotal, as it was for Stefan George. But we know already that it was also a kind of delightful game: "Whether one plays with green, lilac, and blue stones or whether one writes poetry, it's all the same, one has the same feeling of happiness, because one can't see the world any more vividly through ecstasy than through bits of [colored] glass."[194] She metaphorized her writing habits like this: "I write for myself primarily, let everything I've written get hard like an earth, like a star that becomes earth. Then I take the earth in my hand and play ball with it."[195] Translated into everyday reality, this suggests that the poetess, after an initial flow of associations, put her creations aside and later perhaps rearranged the parts—phrases, sentences, or strophes. In many poems the array of images is conceivably commutable; the pieces could be "played" in a different sequence; but, of course, each arrangement results in differently felt emphases in the experience. Very likely the composition is not by chance. We know that Lasker-Schüler worked over and revised her poems continuously, often long after their original publication. Compare, for example, the two versions of "My Quiet Song."

Lasker-Schüler rejected the intrusion of external "purpose" into art: "I almost slapped [Stefan] George on the street"—although on an earlier occasion she had approached and wordlessly given him a flower—"I was so disappointed. Affected people! Art shouldn't educate but crown with garlands."[196] She was also distrustful of Hugo von Hofmannsthal's gracefully perfect form, especially of his *Jedermann*'s didactic intent.[197] Her own poetic labors were mainly in praise of others or were lamentations on the sorrows of the self.

Art was reception of God; it was a game with colored stones; but certainly it was not to be an exercise in intellectual or spiritual vanity, a public preening of one's feathers. Schalom Ben-Chorin reports that she did not like self-conscious talk about artistic matters, preferring to discuss—it sounds quite curious—politics.[198] She once exclaimed, "You wouldn't believe how literary topics revolt me, that pluck to pieces and plunder the game, the charms of the soul. I am so alone, so barren inwardly that I scorn every sensation, every immodesty."[199] A café friend whom she dubbed Cajus-Majus, Caesar of Rome, provoked her to the outburst: "If he only weren't always talking about literature! As long as it's my verses it's okay, but when he begins to blather about Aristophanes, let Dante's Inferno fetch him."[200]

13.

Some of her critics wish that she had been less reluctant to think about questions of taste. In the end we must also face those critical doubts that even sympathy never spared her. The most frequent charges are: kitsch, monotony, defective workmanship—all of them true to a degree.

Marianne Lienau, one of Else Lasker-Schüler's most unforgiving detractors, but not the only one, decries her "cutesy kitsch" (*neckischer Kitsch*), deplores her lack of self-criticism, and deprecates her "calamitous teen-ager tone" (*fataler Backfischton*).[201] Apparently on political grounds, Lienau denies a gifted artist the right to say, "I don't know myself";[202] to do so is an asocial self-indulgence. Lasker-Schüler makes a cult of her Self without examining how this Self reflects her social being. She should have learned to distinguish between kitsch and real sweetness, gaiety and silliness, originality of language and buffoonery.[203]

Perhaps Lasker-Schüler was herself regretting a certain sentimental indecisiveness of mind when she noted, "The teeth have fallen out of my thoughts, I think too sweetly,"[204] yet this very image shows how her uncontrolled associations can forge incisive language. The boundary between sentimentality and rapture is a fine one, as Schlocker admits,[205] and not only the poet but also the reader may misjudge it subjectively. One might contend that it is best to avoid these swampy borderlands of feeling. For good or ill, however, poets tend to wander quite heedlessly through all the territory they inhabit. Lasker-Schüler's realm verged on the marshes of sentiment, that much is clear, and she inevitably sometimes crossed the line. Most readers will recognize this wavering boundary *within* her work, even within particular poems, without confining her finally to either side.

Her images, rhythms, and sentiments are sometimes repetitive. Bänsch detects a "wearying stereotypy,"[206] and for Schlocker she fails to escape the "danger of playing with the worn-out coins of words."[207] Particularly in the two- and three-line stanzas, Lasker-Schüler's rhythmic style can ring repetitive because of the predominant conjoining of brief rhythmic and syntactic periods, their brevity being the (negative) operative factor. When, in addition, the images are picked from her staple stock of favorite "stones" or "buttons"—words like *star, blue, gold*—an individual poem may not come alive, especially if read in company with others that use the same repertoire. Of course, countless other poets have cultivated personal mannerisms or rethreshed empty grain—one thinks of Trakl immediately or even Heine—but what poet has not? The greatest poets will be the most continuous fountains of innovation; the merely good ones will be graced with a score of poems in which their genius springs to life, while the rest of their works may be respectfully shelved like significant scraps from the atelier, clues to the designs perfected in the best.

Her critics have begrudged the embattled poetess even these few perfected poems, though this is surely less easy to understand. Pörtner judges himself as a critic, rather than her as a poet, when he

Else Lasker-Schüler 49

concludes: "I don't know any perfect poem by her. . . . When I seek in my memory I find words, series of words, verses of poems, but no poems."[208] And Schlocker: "It is not given to the poem to reach ripeness" under Lasker-Schüler's hand.[209] Or Heselhaus: "The literary significance of Lasker-Schüler lies in the individual pearls of the metaphors."[210] It has become a repetitive cliché in its own right to describe Lasker-Schüler's poems as fragmentary and without logical development. Yet, although some poems may be circular "garlands of praise," the best progressively evoke their subject and build to a rhetorical climax. It is difficult to see how this simple fact can be overlooked.

Beginning with "Spring," one can go on to name "Old Spring," "Then," "Weltschmerz," "Viva!," "Fortissimo," and "Youth," in *Styx* alone, as not necessarily great poems, but yet as developed, rounded, in their own way unflawed works. And who could carelessly deny the truly completed beauty of "Reconciliation," "Pharaoh and Joseph," "A Song of Love," "To the Barbarian," "A Song," "Georg Trakl," "My Quiet Song" (second version), "Prayer," "Abraham and Isaac," "Moses and Joshua," "David and Jonathan," "Esther," "Genesis," "To My Child," "My Blue Piano," "Chased Away," or "A Love Song"?

The thematic range of these songs is narrow, if the forces of love and dejection can be thought of as limited, but the sentiments ring true, and the music is haunting and original. Solipsistic Lasker-Schüler may have been—eccentric, careless, paranoid, in some respects selfish. Yet the powerful glow of her eros holds transfixed for us in its beam the figures of long-forgotten people—people more practical than she, more selfless, less distracted, less anxious, less afraid of death, who did not jingle their cheap jewelry in others' faces, and who did not die with little left so far from home.

Where are they now, though?

In these few poems.

Notes

The abbreviations in the notes indicate the following works:

CH = Clemens Heselhaus. *Deutsche Lyrik der Moderne*. Düsseldorf, 1962.
DB = Dieter Bänsch. *Else Lasker-Schüler: Zur Kritik eines etablierten Bildes*. Stuttgart, 1971.
DD = Else Lasker-Schüler. *Dichtungen und Dokumente*, ed. Ernst Ginsberg. Munich, 1951.
FM = Fritz Martini. "Else Lasker-Schüler. Dichtung und Glaube." In *Der deutsche Expressionismus: Formen und Gestalten*, ed. Hans Steffen. Göttingen, 1965.
GB = Gottfried Benn. *Gesammelte Werke*, Vol. 4. Wiesbaden, 1968.
GS = Georges Schlocker. "Else Lasker-Schüler." In *Expressionismus: Gestalten einer literarischen Bewegung*, eds. H. Friedmann and O. Mann. Heidelberg, 1956.
GW = Else Lasker-Schüler. *Gesammelte Werke*. 3 vols. Munich, 1962.
HB = Horst Bienek. "Else Lasker-Schüler." In *Triffst du nur das Zauberwort*, ed. Jürgen Petersen. Frankfurt/M, 1961.
HC = Hans W. Cohn. *Else Lasker-Schüler: The Broken World*. Cambridge, England, 1974.
JC = J. E. Cirlot. *A Dictionary of Symbols*. New York, 1962.
KK = Else Lasker-Schüler. *Briefe an Karl Kraus*, ed. Astrid Gehlhoff-Claes. Cologne-Berlin, n.d. Appended is a "Versuch einer biographischen Darstellung" by Gehlhoff-Claes.
KL = *Kleines literarisches Lexikon*, ed. W. Kayser. Bern, 1953.
MK = Margarete Kupper. "Lebenslauf," In Else Lasker-Schüler, *Sämtliche Gedichte*. Munich, 1966.
MS = Michael Schmid, ed. *Else Lasker-Schüler: Ein Buch zum 100. Geburtstag*. Wuppertal, 1969.
SB = Sigrid Bauschinger. *Else Lasker-Schüler: Ihr Werk und ihre Zeit*. Heidelberg, 1980.
WM = Walter Muschg. *Von Trakl zu Brecht: Dichter des Expressionismus*. Munich, 1961.

1. KL 383.
2. GB 1102: Benn.
3. HC 35: Cohn.
4. FM 6: Martini.
5. MS 164: Peter Hille.
6. FM 22: Martini.
7. HC 109: Cohn.
8. HB 189: Bienek.

9. HB 194: Bienek.
10. DB 227: Hans Benzmann.
11. DB 227: Benzmann.
12. DB 202: Helmut Kreuzer.
13. DB 157: Emerich Reeck.
14. DB 162: Bänsch.
15. MS 186: Kurt Hiller.
16. KK 165: *Rhein. Westf. Zeitung*, 6 July 1911.
17. DB 167: Karl Kraus.
18. MS 189: Paul Pörtner.
19. MS 44: Teo Otto.
20. MS 163: Kraus.
21. KK 165: Heinrich Binder.
22. GW II, 406.
23. GW II, 403.
24. KK 72.
25. KK 67.
26. KK 69.
27. KK 74.
28. MS 88.
29. GB 1102.
30. DB 206.
31. MS 90: Armin T. Wegner.
32. MS 61: Schalom Ben-Chorin.
33. GW II, 689.
34. MS 102: Marianne Lienau.
35. MS 46: Teo Otto.
36. MS 118: Horst Laube.
37. MS 96: Wegner.
38. HC 61.
39. CH 217.
40. MK 306.
41. MS 70: Benn.
42. GS 146.
43. DB 212.
44. GW II, 356.
45. GW II, 388.
46. KK 90.
47. DB 155ff. A critical account of the entire birth-date question.
48. HC 19.
49. GW II, 597.
50. GW II, 745.
51. MK 295.
52. MS 62: Ben-Chorin.
53. GW II, 373.
54. GW II, 423.
55. DB 164.
56. GW II, 518.
57. GW II, 518.
58. FM 17.
59. DB 193.
60. SB 28.
61. DB 195.
62. DB 196.
63. DB 196.
64. GW II, 738.
65. MS 160: Gerhart Werner.
66. MS 164.
67. DB 199ff; following details from Bänsch.
68. KK 157.
69. KK 167.
70. KK 167: Gehlhoff-Claes.
71. DD 579.
72. KK 84.
73. KK 177.
74. GW II, 754.
75. SB 193.
76. HC 97.
77. HC 31; *Die Fackel*, No. 313–14 (Dec. 1910).
78. GW II, 227–28.
79. HC 27; GW II, 401.
80. GW II, 401.
81. GW II, 401–2.
82. CH 227.
83. HC 28.
84. HC 26.
85. HC 27.
86. KK 78.
87. KK 160.
88. GW II, 395, 397.
89. MS 51: Paul Goldscheider.

90. HC 29.
91. GW III, 160.
92. MK 302.
93. KK 90.
94. HC 32.
95. MK 306–7.
96. MS 186: Paul Pörtner.
97. HB 188.
98. GW II, 321.
99. GW II, 366.
100. HC 6.
101. FM 7.
102. MS 122.
103. DB 147, 145.
104. MS 108, 109.
105. GW II, 167.
106. HC 96.
107. HC 38.
108. HC vii–viii.
109. GW II, 387.
110. GW II, 366.
111. MS 191.
112. KK 20; MS 197, 106.
113. GW II, 387.
114. KK 78–79.
115. DD 579.
116. GW II, 742.
117. GW II, 712.
118. HC 104.
119. HC 105.
120. HC 73; DD 576: von Radecki.
121. GW II, 545.
122. MS 62: Ben-Chorin.
123. HC 120.
124. FM 6.
125. GS 144: Schlocker.
126. DB 22: Bänsch.
127. GS 147: Schlocker.
128. DB 25: Bänsch.
129. FM 18: Martini.
130. DB 31: Bänsch.
131. DB 26–27.
132. MS 71: Ben-Chorin.
133. DB 24.
134. GW II, 519.
135. HC 39.
136. WM 142, 75.
137. GS 142.
138. GW II, 147.
139. GW II, 150, 147.
140. GW II, 148.
141. GW II, 146.
142. GW II, 151.
143. JC 295.
144. HC 49, 143.
145. GS 145.
146. JC 50–54.
147. HC 40, 62.
148. HC 40.
149. JC 114, 50–54.
150. DB 115.
151. HC 123.
152. FM 17.
153. DB 109.
154. GW II, 687.
155. HC 118.
156. HC 123.
157. DD 579: von Radecki.
158. GW II, 750.
159. GW II, 750, 150.
160. GW II, 149.
161. GW II, 740.
162. GW II, 727.
163. GW II, 727.
164. DB 129.
165. GW II, 687.
166. HC 149–50.
167. DB 116.
168. KK 74.
169. GW II, 742.
170. GW II, 740.
171. GW II, 742.
172. GW II, 778.

173. GW II, 738.
174. KK 58.
175. KK 76.
176. KK 77.
177. KK 52; GW II, 399.
178. KK 80.
179. GW II, 403.
180. GW II, 387.
181. GW II, 373.
182. DD 515.
183. HC 53.
184. GW II, 402.
185. GW II, 402.
186. KK 88.
187. GW II, 387.
188. DB 119.
189. GW II, 546.
190. GW II, 944.
191. MS 187.

192. GW II, 356.
193. KK 21.
194. KK 11.
195. KK 18.
196. KK 82.
197. KK 137–38.
198. MS 58.
199. KK 89.
200. GW II, 295.
201. MS 105, 106.
202. MS 110.
203. MS 107.
204. KK 20.
205. GS 150.
206. DS 113.
207. GS 143.
208. MS 187.
209. GS 144.
210. CH 228.

Poems by
Else Lasker-Schüler

WELTFLUCHT

Ich will in das Grenzenlose
  Zu mir zurück,
Schon blüht die Herbstzeitlose
  Meiner Seele,
Vielleicht—ist's schon zu spät zurück!
O, ich sterbe unter Euch!
Da Ihr mich erstickt mit Euch.
Fäden möchte ich um mich ziehn—
Wirrwarr endend!
  Beirrend,
Euch verwirrend,
  Um zu entfliehn
    Meinwärts!

FRÜHLING

Wir wollen wie der Mondenschein
Die stille Frühlingsnacht durchwachen,
Wir wollen wie zwei Kinder sein,
Du hüllst mich in Dein Leben ein
Und lehrst mich so, wie Du, zu lachen.

Ich sehnte mich nach Mutterlieb'
Und Vaterwort und Frühlingsspielen,
Den Fluch, der mich durch's Leben trieb,
Begann ich, da er bei mir blieb,
Wie einen treuen Feind zu lieben.

Nun blühn die Bäume seidenfein
Und Liebe duftet von den Zweigen.
Du mußt mir Mutter und Vater sein
Und Frühlingsspiel und Schätzelein!
—Und ganz mein Eigen . . .

FLIGHT FROM THE WORLD

I want to go back into boundlessness,
    Return to me.
Already the timeless crocus of my soul
    Blossoms autumnally;
Perhaps—it's too late to return!
Oh, I perish here among you!
For you smother me with your selves.
I'd like to spin threads around me—
End the disorder!
    Vex you,
Perplex you,
    So I can flee
        Mewards!

SPRING

Now like the moonlight let us stray
And wake the quiet spring night through—
Now like two children let us play;
Your warming life about me lay,
And teach me how to laugh like you.

I long had yearned for a mother's love,
A father's word, and springtimes merry;
The curse that me forever drove—
Since it wouldn't leave—I learned to love,
With time, like a true adversary.

Now silken trees are blossoming,
And twigs pour out love's fragrance sweetly.
You'll do my mother-and-fathering,
Be lovey-dove and games of spring!
—And mine completely . . .

TRIEB

Es treiben mich brennende Lebensgewalten,
Gefühle, die ich nicht zügeln kann,
Und Gedanken, die sich zur Form gestalten,
Fallen mich wie Wölfe an!

Ich irre durch duftende Sonnentage . . .
Und die Nacht erschüttert von meinem Schrei.
Meine Lust stöhnt wie eine Marterklage
Und reisst sich von ihrer Fessel frei.

Und schwebt auf zitternden, schimmernden Schwingen
Dem sonn'gen Thal in den jungen Schoss,
Und läßt sich von jedem Mai'nhauch bezwingen
Und giebt der Natur sich willenlos.

INSTINCT

The burning forces of life propel me,
Feelings that I cannot restrain;
And thoughts that suddenly take shape
Attack like wolf packs on the plain.

I stray through the fragrant, sunny days,
And the night is shattered by my cry.
My pleasure moans like a tortured groan
And breaks its fetters with a sigh.

And hovers on trembling, shimmering wings
To the valley's lap—bright, young, and free,
And succumbs to the mastery of each May breath
And surrenders to Nature will-lessly.

URFRÜHLING

Sie trug eine Schlange als Gürtel
Und Paradiesäpfel auf dem Hut,
Und meine wilde Sehnsucht
Raste weiter in ihrem Blut.

Und das Ursonnenbangen,
Das Schwermüt'ge der Glut
Und die Blässe meiner Wangen
Standen auch ihr so gut.

Das war ein Spiel der Geschicke
Ein's ihrer Rätseldinge . . .
Wir senkten zitternd die Blicke
In die Märchen unserer Ringe.

Ich vergass meines Blutes Eva
Ueber all' diesen Seelenklippen,
Und es brannte das Rot ihres Mundes,
Als hätte ich Knabenlippen.

Und das Abendröten glühte
Sich schlängelnd am Himmelssaume,
Und vom Erkenntnisbaume
Lächelte spottgut die Blüte.

OLD SPRING

She wore a serpent as girdle;
On her hat, fruit of paradise;
And my own wild rage of yearning
In her blood, too, did rise.

And the sun's age-old terror,
The melancholy of fire,
My own cheek's pallor,
Her also did well attire.

That was a game of destinies,
One of their mystery things . . .
Trembling, we dropped our glances
Into the fairy-tales of our rings.

I forgot Eve's blood-born yearning
Over all my soul's steep cliffs,
And the red of her mouth was burning
As if I had boys' lips.

And the blushing glow of evening
Snaked around heaven's hood,
And the buds of the tree of Eden
Smiled ridiculously good.

MAIROSEN
(Reigenlied für die großen Kinder)

Er hat seinen heiligen Schwestern versprochen,
Mich nicht zu verführen,
Zwischen Mairosen hätte er fast
   Sein Wort gebrochen,
Aber er machte drei Kreuze
Und ich glaubte heiss zu erfrieren.

Nun lieg' ich im düst'ren Nadelwald,
Und der Herbst saust kalte Nordostlieder
Ueber meine Lenzglieder.

Aber wenn es wieder warm wird,
Wünsch' ich den heiligen Schwestern beid'
   Hochzeit
Und wir—spielen dann unter den Mairosen . . .

DANN

. . . Dann kam die Nacht mit Deinem Traum
Im stillen Sternebrennen.
Und der Tag zog lächelnd an mir vorbei,
Und die wilden Rosen atmeten kaum.

Nun sehn' ich mich nach Traumesmai,
Nach Deinem Liebeoffenbaren.
Möchte an Deinem Munde brennen
Eine Traumzeit von tausend Jahren.

MAY ROSES
(Roundelay for Big Children)

To his sanctified sisters he pledged as how
He would not seduce me.
Twixt the May roses he just might have
  Broken his vow;
But he thrice made the sign of the cross
And I felt the heat freeze me profusely.

Now in the gloomy pines I lie,
And the Autumn's chill northeast-songs sing
Over my limbs of spring.

But when it once turns warm again,
I hope that the sanctified sisters won't tarry
  To marry
And we—will play then under the roses of May . . .

THEN

. . . Then came the night and brought your dream
In the quiet blaze of stars.
And the smiling day went marching by
Where the wild, breathless roses are.

I long now for a May of dreams,
The moment when your love appears.
I'd like to blaze upon your mouth
A dream-time of a thousand years.

KARMA

Hab' in einer sternlodernden Nacht
Den Mann neben mir um's Leben gebracht.

Und als sein girrendes Blut gen Morgen rann,
Blickte mich düster sein Schicksal an.

SINNENRAUSCH

Dein sünd'ger Mund ist meine Totengruft,
Betäubend ist sein süsser Atemduft,
Denn meine Tugenden entschliefen.
Ich trinke sinnberauscht aus seiner Quelle
Und sinke willenlos in ihre Tiefen,
Verklärten Blickes in die Hölle.

Mein heißer Leib erglüht in seinem Hauch,
Er zittert, wie ein junger Rosenstrauch,
Geküsst vom warmen Maienregen.
—Ich folge Dir ins wilde Land der Sünde
Und pflücke Feuerlilien auf den Wegen,
—Wenn ich die Heimat auch nicht wiederfinde . . .

KARMA

In a night of stars all blazing free
I killed the man who was next to me.

And as his murmuring blood ran toward the dawn
His fate stared at me baleful and withdrawn.

SENSUAL ECSTASY

Your sinful mouth's my burial crypt,
Narcotic in its sweetness, fragrant-lipped,
So that my virtues fell asleep.
I drink with drunken senses from its well
And will-lessly sink down into its deep,
With radiant gaze descending into hell.

Under its breath my body hotly glows;
It quivers like a youthful rose,
Kissed by the warming rain of May.
—With you to the land of sin I'll wildly roam
And pluck up fire lilies by the way
—Even if I never find the road back home.

SEIN BLUT

Am liebsten pflückte er meines Glückes
   Letzte Rose im Maien
Und würfe sie in den Rinnstein.
   . . . Sein Blut plagt ihn.

Am liebsten lockte er meiner Seele
   Zitternden Sonnenstrahl
In seine düst're Nächtequal.

Am liebsten griff er mein spielendes Herz
   Aus wiegendem Lenzhauch
Und hing es auf wo an einem Dornstrauch.
   . . . Sein Blut plagt ihn.

HIS BLOOD

He'd really prefer to pluck my joy's
   Last rose in Maytime
And throw it in the gutter slime.
   . . . His blood torments him.

He'd really prefer to lure my soul's
   Quivering sunbeam
Into his nighttime's tortured dream.

He'd really prefer to snatch my playful heart
   From the spring's cradling air,
And hang it in a bramble-bush somewhere.
   . . . His blood torments him.

VIVA!

Mein Wünschen sprudelt in der Sehnsucht meines Blutes
Wie wilder Wein, der zwischen Feuerblättern glüht.
Ich wollte, Du und ich, wir wären eine Kraft,
Wir wären eines Blutes
Und ein Erfüllen, eine Leidenschaft,
Ein heisses Weltenliebeslied!

Ich wollte, Du und ich, wir würden uns verzweigen,
Wenn sonnentoll der Sommertag nach Regen schreit
Und Wetterwolken bersten in der Luft!
Und alles Leben wäre unser Eigen;
Den Tod selbst rissen wir aus seiner Gruft
Und jubelten durch seine Schweigsamkeit!

Ich wollte, dass aus unserer Kluft sich Massen
Wie Felsen aufeinandertürmen und vermünden
In einen Gipfel, unerreichbar weit!
Dass wir das Herz des Himmels ganz erfassen
Und uns in jedem Hauche finden
Und überstrahlen alle Ewigkeit!

Ein Feiertag, an dem wir ineinanderrauschen,
Wir beide ineinanderstürzen werden,
Wie Quellen, die aus steiler Felshöh' sich ergiessen
In Wellen, die dem eignen Singen lauschen
Und plötzlich niederbrausen und zusammenfliessen
In unzertrennbar, wilden Wasserheerden!

VIVA!

My wishes sparkle in the longing of my blood
Like the wild wine through glowing branches swirls.
I wish that, you and I, we were a single power,
We were a single blood
And one fulfillment, one passionate hour,
One ardent love song of all the worlds.

I wish that, you and I, we could be branched together
When mad with sun the summer day cries out for rain,
And thunder clouds are shattering in the air!
And life belonged to us two altogether;
Then, Death himself we'd snatch out of his lair
And celebrate his silence with disdain.

I wish that boulders rose from our abyss
Like cliffs piled on each other, and would flow
Up to a mountain peak unreachably far!
That we the heart of heaven might firmly seize
And find ourselves in all the winds that blow
And shine over all eternities that are.

A holiday, when together we rush along
And, drunken, into each other both will fall
Like streams that plunge from steep and rocky peaks
In waves that listen only to their own song
And suddenly roar downward, flowing to meet
Inseparably—in a wild white waterfall.

CHAOS

Die Sterne fliehen schreckensbleich
Vom Himmel meiner Einsamkeit,
Und das schwarze Auge der Mitternacht
Starrt näher und näher.

Ich finde mich nicht wieder
In dieser Todverlassenheit!
Mir ist: ich lieg' von mir weltenweit
Zwischen grauer Nacht der Urangst . . .

Ich wollte, ein Schmerzen rege sich
Und stürze mich grausam nieder
Und riß mich jäh an mich!
Und es lege eine Schöpferlust
Mich wieder in meine Heimat
   Unter der Mutterbrust.

Meine Mutterheimat ist seeleleer,
Es blühen dort keine Rosen
Im warmen Odem mehr.—
. . . . Möcht einen Herzallerliebsten haben!
Und mich in seinem Fleisch vergraben.

CHAOS

The stars are fleeing pale with dread
From the heavens of my solitude,
And the black eye of midnight
Stares closer and closer.

I cannot find myself again
In this dead abandonment!
It's as if: I lie world-far from me
Among gray night of old anxiety.

I wish a pain would stir
And hurl me down cruelly
And jerk me to myself!
And some shaping desire
Would lay me down, back home, at rest
   Under my mother's breast.

My motherland is empty-souled;
Roses no longer blossom there
In the warm air—
. . . . If I but had the sweetheart of my wish!
I'd bury myself in his flesh.

VERDAMMNIS

Krallen reissen meine Glieder auf
Und Lippen nagen an meinem Traumschlaf.
Weh Deinem Schicksal und dem meinen,
Das sich im Zeichen böser Sterne traf.
Meine Sehnsucht schreit zu diesen Sternen auf
Und erstarrt im Morgenscheinen—
    Und ich weine
    Zu den Höllen.

Schenk' mir Deine Arme eine Nacht,
Die so frischen Odem strömen
Wie zwei nordische Meereswellen.
Dass, wenn ich aus Finsternis erwacht,
Mich nicht böse Geister treten,
Ich nicht einsam bin mit meinem Grämen.
Zu den Himmeln fleh' ich jede Nacht,
Doch der Satan hetzt die Teufel auf mein Beten.

WELTSCHMERZ

Ich, der brennende Wüstenwind,
Erkaltete und nahm Gestalt an.

Wo ist die Sonne, die mich auflösen kann,
Oder der Blitz, der mich zerschmettern kann!

Blick' nun: ein steinernes Sphinxhaupt,
Zürnend zu allen Himmeln auf.

Hab' an meine Glutkraft geglaubt.

DAMNATION

My limbs are ripped apart by claws
And lips gnaw at my dreaming sleep.
Woe to your destiny, and my own
That their star-crossèd rendezvous did keep.
My longing cries aloud up to these stars
And in the morning light turns stone—
    And I groan
        To all the hells.

Give me your arms as a gift for a night,
Which such fresh fragrance breathe,
Like two Nordic ocean swells.
So when I wake from my dark night
Demons won't trample my despair,
So I'll not be alone with grief.
To the heavens I send my plea each night.
But Satan sets his devils on my prayer.

WELTSCHMERZ

I, the burning desert wind
Grew cold and took on form.

Where is the sun that can dissolve
Or the lightning that can smash me!

Look now: a stone Sphinx head
Raging to all the heavens.

I believed in the power of my fire.

MEIN DRAMA

Mit allen duftsüssen Scharlachblumen
Hat er mich gelockt,
Keine Nacht mehr hielt ich es im engen Zimmer aus,
Liebeskrumen stahl ich mir vor seinem Haus
Und sog mein Leben, ihn ersehnend, aus.
Es weint ein blasser Engel leis' in mir
Versteckt—ich glaube tief in meiner Seele,
    Er fürchtet sich vor mir.
Im wilden Wetter sah ich mein Gesicht!
Ich weiß nicht wo, vielleicht im dunklen Blitz,
Mein Auge stand wie Winternacht im Antlitz,
Nie sah ich grimmigeres Leid.
. . . Mit allen duftsüssen Scharlachblumen
  Hat er mich gelockt,
Es regt sich wieder weh in meiner Seele
Und leitet mich durch all' Erinnern weit.
Sei still, mein wilder Engel mein,
    Gott weine nicht
  Und schweige von dem Leid,
Mein Schmerzen soll sich nicht entladen,
Keinen Glauben hab' ich mehr an Weib und Mann,
Den Faden, der mich hielt mit allem Leben,
Hab' ich der Welt zurückgegeben
    Freiwillig!
Aus allen Sphinxgesteinen wird mein Leiden brennen,
Um alles Blühen lohen, wie ein dunkler Bann.
Ich sehne mich nach meiner blind verstoss'nen Einsamkeit,
Trostsuchend, wie mein Kind, sie zu umfassen,
Lernte meinen Leib, mein Herzblut und ihn hassen,
    Nie so das Evablut kennen
    Wie in Dir, Mann!

MY DRAMA

With all sweet-fragrant scarlet flowers
He lured me;
Not a single night could I stand it in my cramped room;
Before his house I stole me some crumbs of love
And, longing for him, ate my life away.
An angel pale weeps in me silently
Concealed—I think deep in my soul
    He is afraid of me.
In the wild storm I saw my face!
I don't know where, perhaps in a darkening flash,
My eye was a wintry night in my countenance,
I never saw grimmer pain.
. . . With all sweet-fragrant scarlet flowers
  He lured me;
Misery lifts its head in my soul again
And leads me through all distant memory.
Be still, O my wild angel mine,
    Let God not weep
  And speak not of the pain;
My suffering shall not be unleashed;
My faith is lost in man and woman;
The thread that held me to all life
I gave back to the world of strife
    Of my free will!
Out of all Sphinx's stones my pain will burn,
Around all blooming, blaze like a gloomy spell.
I'm longing for my blindly banished loneliness;
Seek comfort, like my child, in its embrace.
Learned hate for my body, my heart's blood and him;
    Never know thus the blood of Eve
    As in you, Man!

FORTISSIMO

Du spieltest ein ungestümes Lied,
Ich fürchtete mich nach dem Namen zu fragen,
Ich wusste, er würde das alles sagen,
Was zwischen uns wie Lava glüht.

Da mischte sich die Natur hinein
In unsere stumme Herzensgeschichte,
Der Mondvater lachte mit Vollbackenschein,
Als machte er komische Liebesgedichte.

Wir lachten heimlich im Herzensgrund,
Doch unsere Augen standen in Thränen
Und die Farben des Teppichs spielten bunt
In Regenbogenfarbentönen.

Wir hatten beide dasselbe Gefühl,
Der Smyrnateppich wäre ein Rasen,
Und die Palmen über uns fächelten kühl,
Und unsere Sehnsucht begann zu rasen.

Und unsere Sehnsucht riss sich los
Und jagte uns mit Blutsturmwellen:
Wir sanken in das Smyrnamoos
Urwild und schrieen wie Gazellen.

FORTISSIMO

You played me an impetuous song;
I trembled to ask what its name might be.
I knew it would tell what all along
Has glowed like lava twixt you and me.

Then Mother Nature came butting in,
In the mute history of our hearts;
The moon-father shone with full-cheeked grin
As if writing comical lovers' parts.

We secretly laughed in our inmost soul,
But still the tears hung in our eyes;
And the shades of the carpet brightly flowed
With rainbow-colored tints and dyes.

Both of us felt the very same;
The Smyrna carpet seemed a lawn,
And the palms above us coolly swayed,
And our desire came raging on.

And our desire came breaking loose
And hunted us in blood-storm swells:
We sank into the Smyrna moss
Gone wild and screaming like gazelles.

DER GEFALLENE ENGEL
(St. Petrus Hille zu eigen)

Des Nazareners Lächeln strahlt aus Deinen Mienen,
Und meine Lippen öffnen sich mit Zagen,
Wie gift'ge Blüten, die dem Satan dienen
Und scheu den Lenzwind nach dem Himmel fragen.
Die heisse Sehnsucht hat mich tief gebräunt,
In kühler Not erstarrte meine Seele,
Ein Wetter stählte mein Gewissen!

Es wachsen Sträucher blütenlos auf meinen Wegen
Wie Schatten, die verbot'ne Thaten werfen,
Und meine Träume tränkt ein blut'ger Regen
Und reizt mit seinem Schein zum Laster meine Nerven.
Die Unschuld hat an meinem Bett geweint,
Und rang und klagte dann um meine Seele
Und pflanzte Trauerrosen um mein Kissen.

Siehst Du den Kettenring an meinem Finger—
Sein Stein erblindete, sein blaues Scheinen,
Vielleicht verlor ihn mal ein Gottesjünger
Auf seinem Pfade hoch in Felsgesteinen.
Und diese roten, feurigen Granaten
Gab mir ein Königgreis für meine Nächte,
Wie heisse Tropfen auf die Schnur gereiht.

Der Sonnenuntergang erzählt im Westen
Von späten Rosen, die ergrauen müssen
Im Herbste unter morschem Laub und Aesten,
Und nichts vom Sonnenglanz des Sommers wissen,
Als Sünderinnen sterben für die Thaten
Der eitelen Natur, die duften möchte
Noch in der späten Winterabendzeit.

Darf ich mit Dir auf weiten Höhen schreiten!
Hand in Hand, Du und ich, wie Kinder . . .
Wenn aus dem Abendhimmel wilde Sterne gleiten
Durch's tiefe Blauschwarz, wie verstoss'ne Sünder,
Und scheu in Gärten fallen, die voll Orchideen
Und stummen Blüten steh'n
In gold'nen Hüllen.

THE FALLEN ANGEL
(For St. Peter Hille)

The smile of the Nazarene beams from your visage,
And my lips are parted in shy hesitation,
Like poisonous flowers that do the devil's bidding,
And ask the spring wind about heaven's elation.
My passionate desire burned me deep brown.
The numbness of chill misery lamed my soul.
My conscience turned to steel in the thunder's throes.

Like shadows that project forbidden deeds
Beside my paths the unflowering bushes grow;
My dreams are drenched in a red rain that bleeds
Exciting my nerves to vice with its bright flow.
At my bedside weeping innocence sat down
And struggled and lamented for my soul
And planted on my pillow a funeral rose.

Here on my finger, do you see the ring—
The jewel's gone blind that once so bluely shone.
Perhaps a disciple lost it, wandering
High on his path along the cliffs of stone.
And look, these garnets, full of a red fire,
A hoary king bequeathed me for my nights,
Like burning drops all strung upon a string.

The sun that's setting in the west can tell
Of the late roses that in fall turn gray;
Under rotten leaf and branch they bid farewell
But of summer's glorious sun have naught to say;
And yet as sinners for their pride expire,
For nature's vain hope to be fragrant still,
Even at the very end of a winter day.

On the broad heights with you—may I go striding!
Hand in hand like children, you and I.
When, out of the evening heaven, wild stars come gliding,
Rejected sinners through the blue-black sky;
And shyly fall in gardens where flowers stand,
With orchids and quiet buds abloom
In a golden grove.

Und in den Kronen schlanker Märchenbäume
Harrt meine Unschuld unter Wolkenflor,
Und meine ersten, holden Kinderträume
Erwachen vor dem gold'nen Himmelsthor.
Und wenn wir einst ins Land des Schweigens gehen,
Der schönste Engel wird mein Heil erfleh'n
Um Deiner Liebe willen.

SELBSTMORD

Wilde Fratzen schneidet der Mond in den Sumpf
    Und dumpf
        Kreist die Welt.
Hätt' ich nur die Welt überstanden!
Damals als wir uns beide fanden
Blickte auch die Natur so gemein,
Aber dann kam der Sonnenschein
Und sang sein Strahlenlied
    Bis über den Norden.

Nun nagt der Maulwurf an Deinem Gebein,
In der Truhe heult die rote Katze.
Ein Kater schlich, sie lustzumorden
Aus vollmondblutendem Abendschein.
Wie die Nacht voll grausamer Sehnsucht blüht!
Der Tod selbst fürchtet sich zu zwei'n
Und kriecht in seinen Erdenschrein,
    Aber—ich pack' ihn mit meiner Tatze!

And in the crowns of fairy-story trees
Under veils of cloud my innocence will wait;
And my first dearest dreams, of childhood days,
Awaken in front of heaven's golden gate.
And when we go one day to the silent land
The fairest angel will save my soul from doom
Because of this your love.

SUICIDE

The moon makes hideous faces in the swamp
    And in dull pomp
    The world spins round.
If only I'd endured its bother!
Long ago when we found each other
Nature, too, peered nastily;
But there was some sunshine then to see
And sang its beaming song
    Beyond the North.

Now the mole's gnawing at your bone;
In the chest, the red cat's wailing.
A tomcat prowled to rape and kill her
Where the full moon bleeding evening shone.
How the night and its cruel yearnings bloom!
Even Death himself's afraid of others
And creeps into his earthen tomb,
But—with my paw I'll nail him.

JUGEND

Ich hört Dich hämmern diese Nacht
An einem Sarg im tiefen Erdenschacht.
Was willst Du von mir, Tod!
Mein Herz spielt mit dem jungen Morgenrot
Und tanzt im Funkenschwarm der Sonnenglut
Mit all den Blumen und der Sommerlust.

Scheer' Dich des Weges, alter Nimmersatt!
Was soll ich in der Totenstadt,
Ich, mit dem Jubel in der Brust!!

YOUTH

Last night I heard your hammer's craft
Building a coffin down in your shaft.
What do you want from me, Death!
My heart plays in the dawn's young breath,
And whirls in the spark-swarm of the sun
With all the flowers and summer fun.

Clear out, old Neverfed!
Why *me* in the City of the Dead,
Me, whose rejoicing's just begun!!

BALLADE
(Aus den sauerländischen Bergen)

Er hat sich
In ein verteufeltes Weib vergafft,
In sing Schwester!

Wie ein lauerndes Katzentier
Kauerte sie vor seiner Thür
Und leckte am Geld seiner Schwielen.

Im Wirtshaus bei wildem Zechgelag
Sass er und sie und zechten am Tag
Mit rohen Gesellen.

Und aus dem roten, lodernden Saft
Stieg er ein Riese aus zwergenhaft
Verkümmerten Gesellen.

Und ihm war, als blicke er weltenweit,
Und sie schürte den Wahn seiner Trunkenheit
Und lachte!

Und eine Krone von Felsgestein,
Von golddurchädertem Felsgestein,
Wuchs ihm aus seinem Kopf.

Und die Säufer kreischten über den Spass.
»Gott verdamm' mich, ich bin der Satanas!«
Und der Wein sprühte Feuer der Hölle.

Und die Stürme sausten wie Weltuntergang,
Und die Bäume brannten am Bergeshang,
Es sang die Blutschande. . . .

Und sie holten ihn um die Dämmerzeit,
Und die Gassenkinder schrie'n vor Freud'
Und bewarfen ihn mit Unrat.

Seitdem spukt es in dieser Nacht,
Und Geister erscheinen in dieser Nacht,
Und die frommen Leute beten.—

BALLAD
(From the Mountains of the Sauerland)

His head has been
Turned by a devil of a woman,
His own sister.

Like a lurking cat
She crouched by the door where he was at
And licked at the coin of his callouses.

At the tavern in wild revelry
They sat and drank for all to see
With rough companions.

And out of the ruby juice that glows,
From the dwarfed and stunted fellows he rose
Like a giant.

And he saw the whole world beneath his gaze,
And she stoked the fire of his drunken craze
And laughed!

And like a crown a cliff of stone,
A gold-veined cliff of stone
Grew from his head.

And all the drunkards began to laugh.
"Goddammit, ah's the Devil hisse'f!"
And the wine spewed the fire of Hell.

And the storms roared like the end of the world,
And flames from the trees on the hillside swirled,
And incest sang. . .

In the dusk they came to take him away
And the urchins yelled in the street, "Hurray!"
And showered him with rubbish.

Since then a spook walks on this night,
And spirits are abroad here on this night,
And the pious people pray—

Sie schmückte mit Trauer ihren Leib,
Und der reiche Schankwirt nahm sie zum Weib,
Gelockt vom Sumpf ihrer Thränen.

—Und der mit der schweren Rotsucht im Blut
Wankt um die stöhnende Dämmerglut
Gespenstisch durch die Gassen,

Wie leidender Frevel,
Wie das frevelnde Leid,
Überaltert dem lässigen Leben.

Und er sieht die Weiber so eigen an,
Und sie fürchten sich vor dem stillen Mann
Mit dem Totenkopf.

KÖNIGSWILLE

Ich will vom Leben der gazellenschlanken
Mädchen mit glühenden Rosengedanken,
Wenn glanzlose Sterne mein Sterbelied singen
Und bleiche Winde durch die Totenstadt weh'n
Und vom Licht mein warmes Leben erzwingen.

Ich will vom Leben der wettergebräunten
Knaben, die nie eine Thräne weinten,
Wenn die Tode vor meinen Herzthoren steh'n
Und mit der Kraft meiner Seele ringen.

Ich will vom Leben der weissen Gluten
Der Sonne und von der Wolke Morgenbluten
Dem quellenden Rot der Himmelsbrust.
Bis meine Lippen sich wieder färben
Und junger Odem durchströmt meine Brust . . .
Ich will nicht sterben!

She decked her body with mourning-dress,
And lured by the swamp of her tearfulness,
The wealthy innkeeper wed her.

—And the one with the red plague in his blood
Staggers in the groaning sunset flood
Like a ghost through the alleys,

Like suffering wickedness,
Like wicked pain,
Too old for life grown dull.

And he looks at the women so curiously
And they fear the quiet man when they see
His head like a skull.

ROYAL WILL

Give me the life of slender girls,
Gazelles with rose-bright thoughts awhirl,
When lusterless stars intone my dirge
And pale winds sweep the city of the dead,
And my warm life from the light of day is purged.

Give me the life of the weather-browned
Boys who will never weep tear nor sound,
When deaths before my heart's door stand
And with my soul's strength struggle hand to hand.

Give me the life of the fiery glow
Of the sun and the clouds' dawn-bleeding show,
The gushing red of heaven's breast.
Until the red of my lips revivify
And a young breath is pulsing through my breast . . .
I will not die!

DIR

Drum wein' ich,
Dass bei Deinem Kuss
Ich so nichts empfinde
Und ins Leere versinken muss.
    Tausend Abgründe
Sind nicht so tief,
Wie diese grosse Leere.
Ich sinne im engsten Dunkel der Nacht,
    Wie ich Dir's ganz leise sage,
Doch ich habe nicht den Mut.
Ich wollte, es käme ein Südenwind,
Der Dir's herüber trage,
Damit es nicht gar voll Kälte kläng'
Und er Dir's warm in die Seele säng'
    Kaum merklich durch Dein Blut.

SCHULD

Als wir uns gestern gegenübersassen,
Erschrak ich über Deine Blässe,
Ueber die Leidenslinie Deiner Wange.
Da kam's, dass meine Gedanken mich vergassen
Ueber der Leidenslinie Deiner Wange.

Es trafen unsere Blicke sich wie Sternenfragen,
Es war ein goldenes Hin- und Herverweben
Und Deine Augen glichen seid'nen Mädchenaugen.
Du öffnetest die Lippen, mir zu sagen. . . .
Und meine Seele färbte sich in Matt,
Dumpf läutete noch einmal Brand mein Leben
Und schrumpfte dann zusammen wie ein Blatt.

TO YOU

I weep because
At your kiss, I confess,
I don't feel anything
And just sink down in emptiness.
    A thousand voids
Are not so deep
As this vast emptiness.
I think in the closest darkness of the night
    How I'll tell you very softly;
Yet I haven't strength to dare.
Would that a wind would come up from the south
To bring you word in flight,
So that it would not sound so full of cold,
Would warmly sing itself into your soul,
    Through your blood scarce aware.

GUILT

When yesterday you sat there facing me
Your paleness caused me great alarm,
Because of the line of suffering on your cheek.
My thoughts forgot my self, surprisingly,
Because of the line of suffering on your cheek.

Our glances met like questions to the stars.
There was a golden weaving back and forth,
And your eyes were like the silken eyes of girls.
Your lips were parted and you tried to say. . . .
And then my soul lost color and went dull-eyed.
Faintly my life rang fire alarm once more
And, like a leaf then, slowly shrank and died.

UNGLÜCKLICHER HASS
(Versrelief)

Du! Mein Böses liebt Dich
Und meine Seele steht
Furchtbarer über Dir,
Wie der drohendste Stern über Herculanum.

Wie eine Wildkatze springt
Mein Böses aus mir,
Und beisst nach Dir.
    Entrissen
Von Liebesküssen
Aber taumelst Du
In Armen bekränzter Hetären
Durch rosenduftender Sphären
    Rauschgesang.

Nachts schleichen Hyänen,
Wie brütende Finsternisse
Hungrig über meine Träume
Im Wutglüh'n meiner Thränen.

NACHWEH

Weisst Du noch als ich krank lag,
    So Gott verlassen—
Da kamst Du,
    Es war am Herbsttag,
Der Wind wehte krank durch die Gassen.

Zwei kalte Totenaugen
Hätten mich nicht so gequält,
Wie Deine Saphiraugen,
Die beiden brennenden Märchen.

UNHAPPY HATE
(Verse Relief)

You! My evil loves you.
And my soul stands
More fearfully above you
Than the threateningest star over Herculaneum.

My evil leaps
Like a wildcat from me.
And snaps at you.
    But snatched away
From kisses' play
You reel
In the arms of wreath-crowned courtesans
Through their rose-scented zones'
    Ecstatic song.

Hyenas slink at night
Hungrily about my dreams
Like brooding darknesses
In my tears' raging light.

AFTER-PAIN

Do you recall as I lay ill
    So God-forlorn—
You came then;
    It was Autumn still,
A sick wind through the streets was borne.

Two cold death's eyes
Would not have tortured me
Like your two sapphire eyes,
Those burning fairy tales.

ELEGIE

Du warst mein Hyazinthentraum,
Bist heute noch mein süssestes Sehnen,
Aber mein Wünschen zittert durch Thränen
Und meine Hoffnung klagt vom Trauereschenbaum.

Tausend Wunschjahre lag ich vor Deinen Knieen,
Meine Gedanken sprudelten wie junge Weine,
Ein Venussehnen lag vor Deinen Knieen!

Zwei Sommer hielten wir uns schwer umfangen,
Ich tauchte in den goldenen Strudel Deiner Schelmenlaunen
Bis aus den späten Nächten unsere Sterbeglocken klangen.

Und Neide schlichen heimlich, ihre Geil zu rächen,
Die Wolken drohten wild wie schwarze Posaunen,
Wir träumten beide einen Schmerzenstraum:
Zwei böse Sterne fielen in derselben Nacht
Und wir erblindeten in ihrem Stechen.

Der erste Blick, der uns zu eins gehämmert,
Er quälte sich bis in die Morgenstunden,
Bis weh das Herz des Ostens aufgedämmert.

Da sprangen alle grausigen Sagen auf,
Träumte nur noch Plagen,
Alle Plagen erdrosselten mich
Und reissende Hasse kamen
Und verheerten
Die Haine unserer jung gestorbenen Liebe.
Und wehrten meiner Seele Flucht zu Gott,
Gramjahre bebte ich hin,
Krankte zurück,
Kein Himmel beugte sich zu meinem Harme!
Durch alle Sümpfe schleift' ich mein verhungert Glück,
Und warf mich müd dem Satan in die Arme.

ELEGY

You were my hyacinthine dream.
Are still today my sweetest longing.
But my wish trembles through tears thronging,
And my hope mourns from the weeping tree.

A thousand wish-years, I lay at your knees.
My thoughts were bubbling like young wines.
A Venus-longing lay before your knees!

Two summers long we held each other captive tight.
I plunged in the golden whirlpool of your roguish whims
Till late our death bells rang out of the night.

And envies sneaked in secret, to revenge their lust;
The clouds were wildly threatening like black trombones;
Both of us dreamed a dream of pain:
In the same night two dread stars fell in flame
And their sharp radiance blinded us.

The glance that hammered us first into one,
It agonized into the morning hours
Till, aching, the East's heart rose up in the dawn.

Then all the dreadful legends bounded up.
I dreamed of merest misery.
All the miseries strangled me,
And rending hates appeared
And ravaged
The groves of our love, which had died young.
And barred my soul's escape to God;
Grief-years I shivered through,
Sickened and fell back;
No heaven bent down to solace my alarm!
Through all the swamps I dragged my starving joy—

And hurled myself exhausted into Satan's arm.

VAGABUNDEN

O, ich wollte in den Tag gehen,
Alle Sonnen, alle Glutspiele fassen,
Muss in trunk'ner Lenzluft untergeh'n
Tief in meinem Rätselblut.
Sehnte mich zu sehr nach dem Jubel!
Dass mein Leben verspiele mit dem Jubel.
Kaum noch fühlt' meine Seele den Goldsinn des Himmels,
Kaum noch sehen können meine Augen,
Wie müde Welle gleiten sie hin.
Und meine Sehnsucht taumelt wie eine sterbende Libelle.

    Giesse Brand in mein Leben!
    Ja, ich irre mit Dir,
Durch alle Gassen wollen wir streifen,
Wenn unsere Seelen wie hungernde Hunde knurren.
An allen Höllen unsere Lüste schleifen,
Und sünd'ge Launen alle Teufel fleh'n
Und Wahnsinn werden uns're Frevel sein,
Wie bunte, grelle Abendlichter surren;
Irrsinnige Gedanken werden diese Lichte sein!
Ach Gott! Mir bangt vor meiner schwarzen Stunde,
Ich grabe meinen Kopf selbst in die Erde ein!

VAGABONDS

Oh, I hoped to go into the day,
Seize all the suns, the play of fire;
I must go down in the drunk spring air,
Deep in my riddling blood.
Too much I yearned for jubilation!
That my life be played away in jubilation.
My soul can barely feel the golden sense of heaven still,
My eyes can barely see.
They roll on like exhausted waves,
And like a dying dragonfly my longing reels.

     Pour fire into my life!
     Yes, I'll go straying with you;
Let's roam through all the narrow streets,
When our souls growl like hungry dogs;
Let's whet our lusts in hellish heats,
And sinful whims implore all devils,
And our outrages will be quite deranged,
Buzzing like dazzling colored lights of eve.
These lights will be our thoughts' mad birth!
Oh God! But I'm afraid of my dark hour;
I'll bury my own head deep in the earth!

DIE BEIDEN

Dem zuckte sein zackiges Augenbrau jäh
Wie der Blitzstrahl einer Winternacht,
Und jener mit dem süssen Weh,
Dem ringenden Eden im Auge,
Mit dem Himmelblond auf der Stirn. . . .

Ich senkte mich in Beide
Wie ein erleuchtendes Gestirn—
Und es war, als sei ich:
Ihnen ihr Blut zu verraten:

Er mit dem scharfen Stahl im Aug'
Träumte von Heldenthaten
Im Dickicht meiner Urwaldaugen.
Und jenem, dem die Höhen des Parnassos
Mit Goldblicken winkten sternenwärts,
Ihm spannte ich zwei meiner wilden,
Ungezähmten Dürste ans Herz.

THE TWO OF THEM

One's jagged eyebrow twitched abruptly
Like lightning on a winter's eve;
And the other one did sweetly grieve,
With a grappling Eden in his eye,
With a blondness on his brow divine. . . .

Down I sank in them both
Like a constellation's shine—
And it seemed as if I were
Meant to betray to them their blood:

He with the gaze of sharpened steel
Dreamed of heroic knightlihood
In the brush of my jungle eyes.
And him, whom the Parnassian heights
With golden glances beckoned to starry parts,
To him I harnessed two of my untamed
Wild thirsts to drive his heart.

MEINE BLUTANGST

Es war eine Ebbe in meinem Blut,
Es schrie wie brüllende Ozeane
Und mit meiner Seele wehte der Tod
Wie mit einer Siegesfahne.

Zehn Könige standen um mein Bett,
Zehn stolze, leuchtende Sterne,
Sie tränkten mit Himmelsthau meine Qual,
Alle Abende meine Erbqual.

Jäh rissen sich ihre Willen los,
Wie schneidende Winterstürme.
Ueber die Herzen hinweg!
Ueber das Leben hinweg!
Und ihr rasender Mut wuchs Türme!
Und sie schlugen meine Blutangst tot,
Wie Himmelsbrand blühte das Morgenrot,
Und mein Blass schneite von ihren Wangen.

THE FEAR DEEP IN MY BLOOD

There was an ebb tide in my blood;
It screamed like the bellowing sea.
And death was waving with my soul
Like a flag of victory.

Ten kings stood round about my bed,
Ten proud and gleaming stars.
With heavenly dew they drenched my agony,
Each evening my ancestral agony.

Suddenly their wills tore away,
Like piercing winter storms.
Over the hearts and away!
Over life and away!
Out of their wild courage towers formed!
And they struck my blood-fear dead;
Like fire in the heavens blossomed the morning red
And from their cheeks my pallor fell like snow.

IM ANFANG
(Weltscherzo)

Hing an einer goldenen Lenzwolke,
Als die Welt noch Kind war,
Und Gott noch junger Vater war.
    Schaukelte, hei!
      Auf dem Ätherei,
        Und meine Wollhärchen flitterten ringelrei.
Neckte den wackelnden Mondgrosspapa,
Naschte Goldstaub der Sonnenmama,
In den Himmel sperrte ich Satan ein
Und Gott in die rauchende Hölle ein.
Die drohten mit ihrem grössten Finger
Und haben »klumbumm! klumbumm!« gemacht
Und es sausten die Peitschenwinde!
Doch Gott hat nachher zwei Donner gelacht
Mit dem Teufel über meine Todsünde.
Würde 10 000 Erdglück geben,
Noch einmal so gottgeboren zu leben,
So gottgeborgen, so offenbar.
     Ja! Ja!
Als ich noch Gottes Schlingel war!

STYX

O, ich wollte, daß ich wunschlos schlief,
Wüßt ich einen Strom, wie mein Leben so tief,
Flösse mit seinen Wassern.

IN THE BEGINNING
(World Scherzo)

I hung on a golden cloud of spring
When the world was still a child,
And God a young father still
   Sat swinging, hey!
   On the ether egg,
   And my woolly hair all flitted a roundelay.
Teased the nodding moon-granddaddy,
Nibbled the gold dust of sun-mamá.
In Heaven I locked Satan in,
And God into smoking Hell I penned.
They threatened with their longest finger
And went: "Hurrump!" "Hurrump!" perhaps,
And the dashing winds came whipping!
But afterwards God laughed two thunderclaps
With the Devil about my mortal sin.
I'd give 10,000 earthly pleasures
To be once more so much God's treasure,
So safe in God, so free and wild.
   Ah yes!
When I was still God's naughty child.

STYX

Oh, I wish that I could wishless sleep;
If I knew a stream that's like my life—so deep.
I'd flow with its waters.

DASEIN

Hatte wogendes Nachthaar,
Liegt lange schon wo begraben.
Hatte Augen wie Bäche klar,
Bevor die Trübsal mein Gast war,
Hatte Hände muschelrotweiß,
Aber die Arbeit verzehrte ihr Weiß.
Und einmal kommt der Letzte,
Der senkt den hohlen Blick
Nach meines Leibes Vergänglichkeit
Und wirft von mir alles Sterben.
Und es atmet meine Seele auf
Und trinkt das Ewige.

LENZLEID

Daß du Lenz gefühlt hast
In meiner Winterhülle,
Daß du den Lenz erkannt hast
In meiner Todstille—
Nicht wahr, das ist Gram
Winter sein, eh der Sommer kam,
Eh der Lenz sich ausgejauchzt hat.

O, du! schenk mir deinen goldenen Tag
Von deines Blutes blühendem Rot.
Meine Seele friert vor Hunger,
Ist satt vom Reif—
O, du! Gieße dein Lenzblut
Durch meine Starre,
Durch meinen Scheintod.
Sieh, ich harre
Schon Ewigkeiten auf dich.

MY BEING

Had billowing night-hair;
Lies long buried somewhere.
Had eyes like brooks, so clear,
Before affliction came to visit.
Had hands like shells of red and white.
But work devoured their white.
And some day the Last One will come;
He'll drop his hollow glance
Toward my body's evanescence,
And from me cast all death.
And then my soul will breathe relief
And drink the eternal.

SPRING SORROW

That you have felt the spring
Beneath my wintry sheath;
That you perceived the spring
In my repose of death—
That's grief—you'd say the same—
That winter's there before the summer came,
Before the spring's exulted to the full.

Ah, Dear! give me your golden day
Of your blood's flowering red.
My soul is freezing from its hunger,
Satiate with frost—
Ah, Dear! Pour in your springtime blood
Through my rigidity,
Through my dull look of death.
See, since eternity
I have been waiting for you.

LIEBESSTERNE

Deine Augen harren vor meinem Leben
Wie Nächte, die sich nach Tagen sehnen,
Und der schwüle Traum liegt auf ihnen unergründet.

Seltsame Sterne starren zur Erde,
Eisenfarbene mit Sehnsuchtsschweifen,
Mit brennenden Armen die Liebe suchen
Und in die Kühle der Lüfte greifen.

SCHWARZE STERNE

Warum suchst du mich in unseren Nächten,
In Wolken des Hasses auf bösen Sternen!
Laß mich allein mit den Geistern fechten.

Sie schnellen vorbei auf Geyerschwingen
Aus längst vergessenen Wildlandfernen.
Eiswinde durch Lenzessingen.

Und du vergißt die Gärten der Sonne
Und blickst gebannt in die Todestrübe.
Ach, was irrst du hinter meiner Not.

LOVE STARS

Your eyes are lingering before my life
Like nights that long for days;
And sultry dreams lie on them, bottomless.

Most curious stars stare at the earth,
Iron-colored, trailing tails of yearning.
They reach into the coolness of the breeze
And seek out love with arms of burning.

BLACK STARS

Why do you look for me in our nights,
In clouds of hate upon wicked stars!
Leave me alone with the ghosts that I fight.

They come darting past me on vulture's wing,
From lands long forgotten, wild and far.
Ice-winds through the singing spring.

And you forget the gardens of the sun
And, spellbound, stare at gloomy death.
Ah, why do you chase my miseries as they run.

ERKENNTNIS

Schwere steigt aus allen Erden auf
Und wir ersticken im Bleidunst,
Jedoch die Sehnsucht reckt sich
Und speit wie eine Feuersbrunst.
Es tönt aus allen wilden Flüssen
Das Urgeschrei, Evas Lied.
Wir reißen uns die Hüllen ab,
Vom Schall der Vorwelt hingerissen,
    Ich nackt! Du nackt!
- -
Wilder, Eva, bekenne schweifender,
Deine Sehnsucht war die Schlange,
Ihre Stimme wand sich über deine Lippe,
Und biß in den Saum deiner Wange.

Wilder, Eva, bekenne reißender,
Den Tag, den du Gott abrangst,
Da du zu früh das Licht sahst
Und in den blinden Kelch der Scham sankst.

Riesengroß
Steigt aus deinem Schoß
Zuerst wie Erfüllung zagend,
Dann sich ungestüm raffend,
    Sich selbst schaffend
    Gott-Seele. . . . .
Und sie wächst
Über die Welt hinaus,
Ihren Anfang verlierend,
Über alle Zeit hinaus,
Und zurück um dein Tausendherz
Ende überragend . . .

Singe, Eva, dein banges Lied einsam,
Einsamer, tropfenschwer wie dein Herz schlägt,
Löse die düstere Tränenschnur,
Die sich um den Nacken der Welt legt.

Wie das Mondlicht wandele dein Antlitz. . . .
Du bist schön. . . .

KNOWLEDGE

A heaviness arises from all earths
And we are strangling in a leaden haze,
And yet old longing lifts its head
And spews forth like a roaring blaze.
There rings from all the rivers wild
The primal cry, the song of Eve.
We tear off every covering veil,
By the primeval sound beguiled.
     I naked! You naked!
- -

Wilder, Eve, confess more excessively
How your longing was the snake;
Its voice went winding across your lip
And bit in the border of your cheek.

Wilder, Eve, confess more impetuously:
You wrestled the day from God and overcame;
When you too early saw the light
And sank into the blinded cup of shame.

Vast in its size
From your womb does arise
First like fulfillment hesitating,
Then gathering in rage,
    Itself creating
      God-soul. . . . . . .
And it grows
Beyond the world,
Lost to its start,
Beyond all time,
And back around your marvelous heart
Overtopping the end . . .

Sing, Eve, your anxious song alone,
Lonelier, heavy-dropped like the heartbeat's song.
Loosen the gloomy string of tears
That around the neck of the world is hung.

Change your countenance like moonlight. . . .
You are very fair. . . .

Singe, singe, horch, den Rauscheton,
Spielt die Nacht auf deinem Goldhaar schon:

»Ich trank atmende Süße
Vom schillernden Aste
Aus holden Dunkeldolden.
Ich fürchte mich nun
Vor meinem wachenden Blick—
Verstecke mich, du—
Denn meine wilde Pein
    Wird Scham,
Verstecke mich, du,
Tief in das Auge der Nacht,
Daß mein Tag Nachtdunkel trage.
Dieses taube Getöse, das mich umwirrt!
Meine Angst rollt die Erdstufen herauf,
Düsterher, zu mir zurück, nachthin,
Kaum rastet eine Spanne zwischen uns.

Brich mir das glühende Eden von der Schulter!
Mit seinen kühlen Armen spielten wir,
Durch seine hellen Wolkenreife sprangen unsere Jubel.
Nun schnellen meine Zehe wie irre Pfeile über die Erde,
Und meine Sehnsucht kriecht in jähen Bogen mir voran.«

Eva, kehre um vor der letzten Hecke noch!
Wirf nicht Schatten mit dir,
Blühe aus, Verführerin.

Eva du heiße Lauscherin,
O, du schaumweiße Traube,
Flüchte um vor der Spitze deiner schmalsten Wimper noch!

Sing, sing, hear the rustling, hear,
The night already plays on your golden hair.

"I drank breathing sweetness
From the shimmering branch
Out of the fair dark flowers.
I am fearful now
Of my waking glance—
Conceal me, dear—
For my savage pain
    Turns to shame.
Conceal me, dear,
Deep in night's eye,
So my day will bear the dark of night.
This deafening roar, pell-mell about me!
My fear rolls up the steps of the earth,
Gloomily hither—back to me—night-hence;
Hardly an inch remains between us.

Break off the glowing Eden from my shoulder!
We played with its cool arms;
Through its bright hoops of cloud our jubilations sprang.
Like crazy arrows now, my toes dart through the earth,
And my desire creeps on ahead in sudden curves."

Eve, turn back, before the final hedge!
Don't cast your shadows;
Quit flowering, seductress.

Eve, you hot hearkener,
O you grape-cluster, white as foam,
Turn and flee from the tip of your narrowest eyelash!

LIEBESFLUG

Drei Stürme liebt ich ihn eher, wie er mich,
Jäh schrien seine Lippen,
Wie der geöffnete Erdmund!
Und Gärten berauschten an Mairegen sich.

Und wir griffen unsere Hände,
Die verlöteten wie Ringe sich;
Und er sprang mit mir auf die Lüfte
Gotthin, bis der Atem verstrich.

Dann kam ein leuchtender Sommertag,
Wie eine glückselige Mutter,
Und die Mädchen blickten schwärmerisch,
Nur meine Seele lag müd und zag.

TRAUM

Der Schlaf entführte mich in deine Gärten,
In deinen Traum—die Nacht war wolkenschwarz umwunden—
Wie düstere Erden starrten deine Augenrunden,
Und deine Blicke waren Härten—

Und zwischen uns lag eine weite, steife
Tonlose Ebene . . .
Und meine Sehnsucht, hingegebene,
Küßt deinen Mund, die blassen Lippenstreife.

FLIGHT OF LOVE

I loved him three storms earlier than he me;
His lips abruptly cried
Like the opening maw of earth!
And gardens became drunk on the rain of May.

And we seized each other's hands;
They were soldered shut like rings.
And he leaped with me on the winds,
Godwards, until our breath gave way.

Then came a luminous summer day
Much like a blissful mother,
And the girls stood gazing rapturously.
Only *my* soul was tired, and afraid to play.

DREAM

My sleep had kidnaped me into your gardens,
Into your dream—the night was wrapped in cloudy black—
Like gloomy earths your eye sockets stared back
And your glance hardened.

And there between us lay a wide and stiff,
A soundless plain . . .
And my desire, surrendering to its pain,
Kisses your mouth, the pale line of your lips.

»TÄUBCHEN,
DAS IN SEINEM EIGNEN BLUTE SCHWIMMT«

Als ich also diese Worte an mich las,
Erinnerte ich mich
Tausend Jahre meiner.

Eisige Zeiten verschollen—Leben vom Leben,
Wo liegt mein Leben—
Und träumt nach meinem Leben.

Ich lag allen Tälern im Schoß,
Umklammerte alle Berge,
Aber nie meine Seele wärmte mich.

Mein Herz ist die tote Mutter,
Und meine Augen sind traurige Kinder,
Die über die Lande gehen.

»Täubchen, das in seinem eigenen Blute schwimmt«.
Ja, diese Worte an mich sind heiße Tropfen,
Sind mein stilles Aufsterben
»Täubchen, das in seinem eigenen Blute schwimmt«.

In den Nächten sitzen sieben weinende Stimmen
Auf der Stufe des dunklen Tors
Und harren.

Auf den Hecken sitzen sie
Um meine Träume
Und tönen.

Und mein braunes Auge blüht
Halberschlossen vor meinem Fenster
Und zirpt.—
»Täubchen, das in seinem eigenen Blute schwimmt«.

"DOVE THAT SWIMS IN ITS OWN BLOOD"

So when I read these words to me,
I recalled
A thousand years of mine.

Ages of ice now vanished—Life from all life,
Where lies my life—
And dreams of my life.

I lay in the womb of all valleys,
Clung to all mountains,
And yet my soul never kept me warm.

My heart is the dead mother,
And my eyes are unhappy children
Who walk across the lands.

"Dove that swims in its own blood."
Yes, these words about me are burning drops,
Are my silent dying-open:
"Dove that swims in its own blood."

In the nights sit seven weeping voices
On the stoop of the dark gate
And wait.

On the hedges they sit
Around my dreams
And sing.

And my brown eye blooms
Half-opened at the window
And chirps—
"Dove that swims in its own blood."

EVA

Du hast deinen Kopf tief über mich gesenkt,
Deinen Kopf mit den goldenen Lenzhaaren,
Und deine Lippen sind von rosiger Seidenweichheit,
Wie die Blüten der Bäume Edens waren.

Und die keimende Liebe ist meine Seele.
O, meine Seele ist das vertriebene Sehnen,
Du liebzitterst vor Ahnungen—
... Und weißt nicht, warum deine Träume stöhnen.

Und ich liege schwer auf deinem Leben,
Eine tausendstämmige Erinnerung,
Und du bist so blutjung, so adamjung ...
Du hast deinen Kopf tief über mich gesenkt—.

UNSER STOLZES LIED

Aber fremde Tage hängen
Über uns mit kühlen Bläuen,
Und weiße Wolkenschollen dräuen,
Das goldene Strahleneiland zu verdrängen.

Auch wir beide sind besiegte Siegerinnen,
Und Kronen steigen uns vom Blut der Zeder,
Propheten waren unsere Väter,
Unsere Mütter Königinnen.

Und süße Schwermutwolken ranken
Sich über ihre Gräber lilaheiß in Liebeszeilen,
Unsere Leiber ragen stolz, zwei goldene Säulen,
Über das Abendland wie östliche Gedanken.

EVE

You bent your head down very close to mine,
Your head with its golden hair of spring;
And your lips are of a rosy and silken softness
Like the buds that the trees of Eden bring.

And my soul is the upsprouting love.
Oh, my soul is the banished longing.
You love-tremble with dark surmise—
. . . And don't know why your dreams lie moaning.

And I lie heavy on your life,
A memory with a thousand stems bestrung;
And you're so fresh, so Adam-young . . .
You bent your head down very close to mine.

OUR PROUD SONG

But alien days hang in suspense
Above us with their cool blues,
And white cloud-clods make threatening moves
To drive away the gold isle's radiance.

We two, too, are beaten victoresses;
From the blood of cedar our crowns arise;
Our fathers they made prophecies,
Our mothers were princesses.

And sweet clouds of melancholy stand
Over their graves hot-lilac in lines of love;
Proudly our bodies, two gold pillars, tower above
Like Eastern thoughts across the Evening Land.

UNSER KRIEGSLIED

Unsere Arme schlingen sich entgegen
Durch das Leben in runden Schwingen,
Durch das Spiel von Feuerringen,
Zwei Äste sich durch Bogenwegen.

Unsere Seelen tragen scharfe Blüten
Und aus ihren Kelchen steigen
Weihedüfte . . . und die Himmel neigen
Ihre Häupter mit den blauen Güten.

Unsere Willen sind zwei harte Degen
Und sie haben nie verfehlt gestritten,
Und wir dringen bis zum Erzkreis vor, in seiner Mitten
Fällt nach dürren Ewigkeiten Freudenregen,

Alles Sehnen nieder, und vor unserm Schilde
Stürzt das blinde Dämmergraugebilde.
Unsere Adern schmettern wie Posaunen!

Unsere Augen blicken sich in Blicken,
Wie zwei Siege sich erblicken—
Und die Nacht des Tages voll in Lichterstaunen.

OUR BATTLE SONG

Our arms go twining out toward one another
Through life in circling swings,
Through the game of fire rings,
Two branches through archways towards each other.

Our souls bloom with sharp flowers
And from their throats arise
Holy incense—and the skies
With goodnesses of blue their great heads lower.

Our wills are two hard swords,
And they have never fought in vain,
And we advance to the brazen circle, where joy's rain
In the midst after dry eternities has poured,

All longing downwards, and before our shields
The blind, gray twilight-figure yields.
Our arteries blare like trombones rent!

Our eyes glance at each other's glances,
Like two victories match glances—
And the day's night full in light-astonishment.

SCHULZEIT

Unter süßem Veilchenhimmel
Ist unsere Liebe aufgegangen,
Und ich suche allerwegen
Nach dir und deinen Morgenwangen.

Und den Ringelrangelhaaren
Rötlichblonden Rosenlocken,
Und den frühlingshellen Augen
Die so frischfreifrohfrohlocken.

Zwischen dicken Gummipflanzen
Lauern hinter Irdentöpfen
Strickpicknadelspitze Augen,
Tücksch aus bitteren Frauenköpfen.

Daß die beiden alten Damen
Hinter unsere Liebe kamen
Und dich in Gewahrsam nahmen,
Sind die Dramen unserer Herzen.

GROTESKE

Seine Ehehälfte sucht der Mond,
Da sonst das Leben sich nicht lohnt.

Der Lenzschalk springt mit grünen Füßen,
Ein Heuschreck über die Wiesen.

Steif steht im Teich die Schmackeduzie,
Es sehnt und dehnt sich Fräulein Luzie.

SCHOOL DAYS

Under the sweet violet skies
Our love was born and grew,
And I've been seeking everywhere
Your cheeks of morn and you.

And your curly-whirly hair,
Reddish-blondish roseate,
And your springtime-brightened eyes
That so joy-jump-jubilate.

Twixt the portly rubber plants
Lurk behind ceramic vases
Knit-pick-needle-pointed eyes,
Spiteful in bitter women's faces.

That the two of those old ladies
Found out what we're thinking of
And took you into custody,
Are the dramas of our love.

GROTESQUE

The moon is looking for his better half;
Without her life's not worth the gaff.

The spring's rogue jumps with feet of green,
A grasshopper across the scene.

Within the pond stands stiff the smackaducy.
Who widens in her longing? Fräulein Lucy.

EVAS LIED

Die Luft ist von gährender Erde herb,
Und der nackte Märzwald sehnt sich
Wie du—o, ich wollte, ich würde der Frühling,
Mit lauter Märchen umblühte ich dich.

Wäre meine Kraft nicht tot!
Ich hab all das Nachleid tragen müssen,
Und mein tagendes Herzrot
Ist von grollenden Himmeln zerrissen.

Und deine Sinne sind kühl,
Und deine Augen sind zwei Morgenfrühen,
Und das Blondgewirr auf deiner Stirn
Glüht, als ob Sonnen sie besprühen.

Aber du bist vertrieben wie ich,
Weil du auf das Land meiner Seele sankst,
Als das Glück des Erkenntnistags aus mir schrie
Und seines Genießens Todangst.

EVE'S SONG

Tart is the air from the earth's fermenting,
And the naked March wood pines and pales
Like you—Oh, I wish I'd become the spring;
I'd flower around you with fairy tales.

If only my strength weren't dead!
All the after-pain I have had to bear,
And my dawning heart-red
The grumbling heavens rip and tear.

And your senses are cool,
And your eyes two mornings, early yet,
And that blond swirl there on your brow
Glows as if suns were spraying it.

But you are banished just like I;
For into the land of my soul you sank from sight
When the joy of my dawning knowledge burst in screams
And the deadly fear of its delight.

MAIENREGEN

Du hast deine warme Seele
Um mein verwittertes Herz geschlungen,
Und all seine dunklen Töne
Sind wie ferne Donner verklungen.

Aber es kann nicht mehr jauchzen
Mit seiner wilden Wunde,
Und wunschlos in deinem Arme
Liegt mein Mund auf deinem Munde.

Und ich höre dich leise weinen,
Und es ist—die Nacht bewegt sich kaum—
Als fiele ein Maienregen
Auf meinen greisen Traum.

MAY RAIN

You wrapped your warming soul
Around my weather-beaten heart;
And all its darker tones,
Far thunders, fade and part.

But it no longer can exult
With its wild injuries,
And, wishless in your arms,
My mouth on your mouth lies.

And I hear you softly weep
And it—the night but barely moves—might seem
As if a May rain fell
Upon my aging dream.

MEIN STILLES LIED

Mein Herz ist eine traurige Zeit,
Die tonlos tickt.

Meine Mutter hatte goldene Flügel,
Die keine Welt fanden.

Horcht, mich sucht meine Mutter,
Lichte sind ihre Finger und ihre Füße wandernde Träume.

Und süße Wetter mit blauen Wehen
Wärmen meine Schlummer

Immer in den Nächten,
Deren Tage meiner Mutter Krone tragen.

Und ich trinke aus dem Monde stillen Wein,
Wenn die Nacht einsam kommt.

Meine Lieder trugen des Sommers Bläue
Und kehrten düster heim.

Verhöhnt habt ihr mir meine Lippe
Und redet mit ihr.

Doch ich griff nach euren Händen,
Denn meine Liebe ist ein Kind und wollte spielen.

Einen nahm ich von euch und den zweiten
Und küßte ihn,

Aber meine Blicke blieben rückwärts gerichtet
Meiner Seele zu.

Arm bin ich geworden
An eurer bettelnden Wohltat.

Und ich wußte nichts vom Kranksein,
Und bin krank von euch,

Und nichts ist diebischer als Kränke,
Sie bricht dem Leben die Füße,

Stiehlt dem Grabweg das Licht,
Und verleumdet den Tod.

MY QUIET SONG
(First Version)

My heart is a sad time
Tonelessly ticking.

My mother had golden wings
That found no world.

Listen! My mother's looking for me;
Her fingers are candles, her feet are wandering dreams.

And sweet weathers with blue winds
Warm my slumber

In the nights always
Whose days are wearing my mother's crown.

And from the moon I drink a quiet wine
When the night comes lonely.

My songs carried the summer's blue
And gloomily turned home.

Scorn you have shown my lip
And speak with it.

But I reached for your hands,
For my love is a child and wanted to play.

One of you I took and then the second
And kissed him.

But my gaze kept turning backward
Toward my soul.

I have become poor
From you begging benefaction.

I knew nothing of illness
And am ill from you.

And nothing's more thievish than illness;
It cripples the feet of life,

Steals light from the path of the grave
And slanders death.

Aber mein Auge
Ist der Gipfel der Zeit,

Sein Leuchten küßt
Gottes Saum.

Und ich will euch noch mehr sagen,
Bevor es finster wird zwischen uns.

Bist du der Jüngste von euch,
So solltest du mein Ältestes wissen.

Auf deiner Seele werden es fortan
Alle Welten spielen.

Und die Nacht wird es wehklagen
Dem Tag.

Ich bin der Hieroglyph,
Der unter der Schöpfung steht.

Und ich artete mich nach euch,
Der Sehnsucht nach dem Menschen wegen.

Ich riß die ewigen Blicke von meinen Augen,
Das siegende Licht von meinen Lippen—

Weißt du einen schwereren Gefangenen,
Einen böseren Zauberer, denn ich.

Und meine Arme, die sich heben wollen,
Sinken . . .

But my eye
Is the pinnacle of time;

Its radiance kisses
The hem of God.

And more, still, will I say to you
Before it turn dark between us.

If you there are the youngest one of you all
Then you should have my oldest wisdom.

From henceforth all the worlds
Will play it on your soul.

And the night will lament it
Unto the day.

I am the hieroglyph
Inscribed beneath creation.

And I assumed your ways
Out of a longing for human kind.

I tore the eternal glances from my eyes.
The light triumphant from my lips—

Do you know a more dangerous prisoner,
A more evil sorcerer than I.

And my arms, that would lift up,
Sink down . . .

MEIN LIEBESLIED

Wie ein heimlicher Brunnen
Murmelt mein Blut,
Immer von dir, immer von mir.

Unter dem taumelnden Mond
Tanzen meine nackten, suchenden Träume,
Nachtwandelnde Kinder,
Leise über düstere Hecken.

O, deine Lippen sind sonnig . . .
Diese Rauschedüfte deiner Lippen . . .
Und aus blauen Dolden silberumringt
Lächelst du . . . du, du.

Immer das schlängelnde Geriesel
Auf meiner Haut
Über die Schulter hinweg—
Ich lausche . . .

Wie ein heimlicher Brunnen
Murmelt mein Blut.

MY LOVE SONG

My blood is a-murmur
Like a secret spring
Always of you. Always of me.

Under the staggering moon
My naked, searching dreams go dancing,
Somnambulant children,
Softly across gloomy hedges.

Oh, your lips are sunny . . .
This drugging fragrance of your lips . . .
And from blue flower clusters, silver-ringed,
You smile . . . ah, you.

Always the serpentine rippling
Over my skin
Across the shoulder and on—
I am listening . . .

My blood is a-murmur
Like a secret spring.

WELTENDE

Es ist ein Weinen in der Welt,
Als ob der liebe Gott gestorben wär,
Und der bleierne Schatten, der niederfällt,
Lastet grabesschwer.

Komm, wir wollen uns näher verbergen . . .
Das Leben liegt in aller Herzen
Wie in Särgen.

Du! wir wollen uns tief küssen—
Es pocht eine Sehnsucht an die Welt,
An der wir sterben müssen.

ANKUNFT

Ich bin am Ziel meines Herzens angelangt.
Weiter führt kein Strahl.
Hinter mir laß ich die Welt,
Fliegen die Sterne auf: Goldene Vögel.

Hißt der Mondturm die Dunkelheit—
. . . O, wie mich leise eine süße Weise betönt . . .
Aber meine Schultern heben sich, hochmütige Kuppeln.

THE END OF THE WORLD

There is a weeping in the world
As if the Good Lord now lay dead,
And, heavy as the grave, the weight
Of the shadow falls like lead.

Come, let's go sneaking off then . . .
In everybody's heart life lies
As in a coffin.

Ah! Let's kiss deeply, you and I—
A longing's knocking at the world
From which we'll surely die.

ARRIVAL

I have arrived at the goal of my heart.
No beam leads farther.
Behind me, I leave the world;
The stars go flying up: Gold birds.

The moon-tower hoists the darkness—
. . . Oh, how softly a sweet tune besounds me . . .
But my shoulders are raised up, haughty domes.

WO MAG DER TOD MEIN HERZ LASSEN?

Immer tragen wir Herz vom Herzen uns zu.
Pochende Nacht
Hält unsere Schwellen vereint.

Wo mag der Tod mein Herz lassen?
In einem Brunnen, der fremd rauscht—

In einem Garten, der steinern steht—
Er wird es in einen reißenden Fluß werfen.

Mir bangt vor der Nacht,
Daran kein Stern hängt.

Denn unzählige Sterne meines Herzens
Vergolden deinen Blutspiegel.

Liebe ist aus unserer Liebe vielfältig erblüht.
Wo mag der Tod mein Herz lassen?

WHERE MIGHT DEATH LEAVE MY HEART?

We always bring each other heart of heart.
The knocking night
Keeps our thresholds joined.

Where might Death leave my heart?
In a spring that gushes strangely—

In a garden that stands like stone—
He'll throw it in a raging river.

I'm afraid of the night
On which no star is hung.

For my heart's numberless stars
Gild the mirror of your blood.

Love variously has blossomed from our love.
Where might Death leave my heart?

LEISE SAGEN—

Du nahmst dir alle Sterne
Über meinem Herzen.

Meine Gedanken kräuseln sich,
Ich muß tanzen.

Immer tust du das, was mich aufschauen läßt,
Mein Leben zu müden.

Ich kann den Abend nicht mehr
Über die Hecken tragen.

Im Spiegel der Bäche
Finde ich mein Bild nicht mehr.

Dem Erzengel hast du
Die schwebenden Augen gestohlen;

Aber ich nasche vom Seim
Ihrer Bläue.

Mein Herz geht langsam unter
Ich weiß nicht wo—

Vielleicht in deiner Hand.
Überall greift sie an mein Gewebe.

SAY IT SOFTLY—

You took for yourself all the stars
Above my heart.

My thoughts are curling;
I have to dance.

You're always doing something that makes me watch,
Just to tire my life.

I cannot carry the evening
Over the hedges any longer.

No more do I find my image
In the mirror of the streams.

You've stolen the archangel's
Floating eyes.

But I nibble on the honey
Of their blueness.

My heart is slowly going down
I don't know where—

Perhaps into your hand;
It snatches at my substance everywhere.

EIN ALTER TIBETTEPPICH

Deine Seele, die die meine liebet,
Ist verwirkt mit ihr im Teppichtibet.

Strahl in Strahl, verliebte Farben,
Sterne, die sich himmellang umwarben.

Unsere Füße ruhen auf der Kostbarkeit,
Maschentausendabertausendweit.

Süßer Lamasohn auf Moschuspflanzenthron,
Wie lange küßt dein Mund den meinen wohl
Und Wang die Wange buntgeknüpfte Zeiten schon.

ICH BIN TRAURIG

Deine Küsse dunkeln, auf meinem Mund.
Du hast mich nicht mehr lieb.

Und wie du kamst—!
Blau vor Paradies;

Um deinen süßesten Brunnen
Gaukelte mein Herz.

Nun will ich es schminken,
Wie die Freudenmädchen
Die welke Rose ihrer Lende röten.

Unsere Augen sind halb geschlossen,
Wie sterbende Himmel—

Alt ist der Mond geworden.
Die Nacht wird nicht mehr wach.

Du erinnerst dich meiner kaum.
Wo soll ich mit meinem Herzen hin?

AN OLD TIBETAN RUG

Both my soul and yours, which loveth mine,
In the Tibetan rug are intertwined.

Ray in ray, infatuated colors,
Stars that heaven-long wooed one another.

On this jewel our feet rest side by side
Thousand-upon-thousand-meshèd wide.

Sweet Lama son upon a musk-plant throne,
How long will your mouth likely kiss my own
And cheek on cheek the brightly knotted times go on.

I AM SAD

Your kisses darken upon my mouth.
You no longer love me.

And when you came—!
Blue from Paradise;

Around your sweetest fountain
My heart tricked and played.

Now I will paint it
Like the daughters of joy
Redden the withered rose of their loins.

Our eyes are halfway closed
Like dying skies—

The moon has become quite old.
No more will the night awaken.

You hardly remember me.
Where shall I turn with my heart?

UND SUCHE GOTT

Ich habe immer vor dem Rauschen meines Herzens gelegen,
Nie den Morgen gesehen,
Nie Gott gesucht.
Nun aber wandle ich um meines Kindes
Goldgedichtete Glieder
Und suche Gott.

Ich bin müde vom Schlummer,
Weiß nur vom Antlitz der Nacht.
Ich fürchte mich vor der Frühe,
Sie hat ein Gesicht
Wie die Menschen, die fragen.

Ich habe immer vor dem Rauschen meines Herzens gelegen;
Nun aber taste ich um meines Kindes
Gottgelichtete Glieder.

AND LOOK FOR GOD

I always lay before my rushing heart,
Never saw the morning,
Never sought God.
But now I wander about my child's
Gold-written limbs
And look for God.

I am weary from slumber;
Know of night's countenance only.
I'm afraid of the dawn;
It has a face
Like people with questions.

I always lay before my rushing heart;
But now I grope about my child's
God-lighted limbs.

HEIMWEH

Ich kann die Sprache
Dieses kühlen Landes nicht,
Und seinen Schritt nicht gehn.

Auch die Wolken, die vorbeiziehn,
Weiß ich nicht zu deuten

Die Nacht ist eine Stiefkönigin.

Immer muß ich an die Pharaonenwälder denken.
Und küsse die Bilder meiner Sterne.

Meine Lippen leuchten schon
Und sprechen Fernes,

Und bin ein buntes Bilderbuch
Auf deinem Schoß.

Aber dein Antlitz spinnt
Einen Schleier aus Weinen.

Meinen schillernden Vögeln
Sind die Korallen ausgestochen,

An den Hecken der Gärten
Versteinern sich ihre weichen Nester.

Wer salbt meine toten Paläste—
Sie trugen die Kronen meiner Väter,
Ihre Gebete versanken im heiligen Fluß.

HOMESICKNESS

I do not understand
The language of this cool land
And cannot keep its pace.

The clouds, too, floating by
I cannot explain.

The night is a step-queen.

I always have to think of the Pharaoh's forests
And kiss the pictures of my stars.

My lips already glow,
Speak distances.

And am a colored picture book
Upon your lap.

But your countenance spins
A veil made of weeping.

The corals are broken out
Of my shimmering birds.

In the hedges of gardens
Their soft nests turn to stone.

Who anoints my dead palaces—
They carried the crowns of my fathers;
Their prayers sank down in the holy stream.

MEINE MUTTER

War sie der große Engel,
Der neben mir ging?

Oder liegt meine Mutter begraben
Unter dem Himmel von Rauch—
Nie blüht es blau über ihrem Tode.

Wenn meine Augen doch hell schienen
Und ihr Licht brächten.

Wäre mein Lächeln nicht versunken im Antlitz,
Ich würde es über ihr Grab hängen.

Aber ich weiß einen Stern,
Auf dem immer Tag ist;
Den will ich über ihre Erde tragen.

Ich werde jetzt immer ganz allein sein
Wie der große Engel,
Der neben mir ging.

MY MOTHER

Was she the great angel
Who walked at my side?

Or does my mother lie buried
Under the sky of smoke—
No blue will ever bloom above her death.

If my eyes only shone with brightness
And brought her light.

Were my smile not sunk in my countenance,
I'd hang it above her grave.

But I know a star
On which it is always day;
This will I carry over her earth.

I will always be quite alone now
Like the great angel
Who walked at my side.

MARIE VON NAZARETH

Träume, säume, Marienmädchen—
Überall löscht der Rosenwind
Die schwarzen Sterne aus.
Wiege im Arme dein Seelchen.

Alle Kinder kommen auf Lämmern
Zottehotte geritten,
Gottlingchen sehen—

Und die vielen Schimmerblumen
An den Hecken—
Und den großen Himmel da
Im kurzen Blaukleide!

MARY OF NAZARETH

Dream and tarry, Mary-maiden,
Everywhere the wind of roses
Quenches the black stars.
Rock in your arms your tiny soul.

All the children come on lambs
Riding giddy-up
To see little godlet—

And the many shimmering flowers
On the hedges—
And the arcing heavens there
In a short dress of blue!

BALLADE
(Zweite Fassung)

Sascha kommt aus Sibirien heim;
Wie er aussehn mag?

Trotzendes Gold seine Stirne war,
Süßer Todstrahl sein Haar,
Seine Lippen brannten am Altar.

Sascha trank meinen Herzseim
Jede Nacht, die am Traumhang lag.

Was er sagen mag—
Wie er klagen mag—

Wo steck ich meinen Liebsten hin?
Da ich ihm untreu war
Und doch nur seine Blume bin.

Dem Dichter färbt er die Schläfe rot,
Seine Ehre sticht den Wilddieb tot.

Aber den König trifft er nicht,
Der hat meines Bruders steinern Gesicht.
Sascha!

BALLAD
(Second Version)

Sascha comes back from Siberia.
What will he look like?

His brow was threatening gold,
His hair a sweet death-ray,
His lips burned on the altar.

Sascha drank my honey-heart
Each night on the hill of dream.

What he will say—
How he'll inveigh—

Where shall I put my dearest one?
Since I was untrue,
And yet I am *his* flower only.

He dyes the poet's temples red;
His honor stabs the poacher dead.

But he doesn't strike the king a blow;
He has my brother's stony brow.
Sascha!

MEIN LIEBESLIED

Auf deinen Wangen liegen
Goldene Tauben.

Aber dein Herz ist ein Wirbelwind,
Dein Blut rauscht, wie mein Blut—

Süß
An Himbeersträuchern vorbei.

O, ich denke an dich—
Die Nacht frage nur.

Niemand kann so schön
Mit deinen Händen spielen,

Schlösser bauen, wie ich
Aus Goldfinger;

Burgen mit hohen Türmen!
Strandräuber sind wir dann.

Wenn du da bist,
Bin ich immer reich.

Du nimmst mich so zu dir,
Ich sehe dein Herz sternen.

Schillernde Eidechsen
Sind deine Geweide.

Du bist ganz aus Gold—
Alle Lippen halten den Atem an.

MY LOVE SONG

Golden doves
Brood upon your cheeks.

But your heart is a whirlwind;
Your blood rushes like my blood—

Sweetly
Past the raspberry bushes.

Oh, I think of you—
Just ask the night.

No one else can play
So nicely with your hands.

Build palaces, like me,
Out of ring finger.

Castles with tall towers!
We're pirates at the beach.

When you are here
I am always rich.

You take me to you so,
I see your heart turn star.

Your entrails are
Lizards of irridescent light.

You are entire of gold—
All lips stop breathing.

EIN LIEBESLIED

Aus goldenem Odem
Erschufen uns Himmel.
O, wie wir uns lieben . . .

Vögel werden Knospen an den Ästen,
Und Rosen flattern auf.

Immer suche ich nach deinen Lippen
Hinter tausend Küssen.

Eine Nacht aus Gold,
Sterne aus Nacht . . .
Niemand sieht uns.

Kommt das Licht mit dem Grün,
Schlummern wir;
Nur unsere Schultern spielen noch wie Falter.

A LOVE SONG

Of golden breath
The heavens shaped us.
Oh, how we love each other . . .

Birds become buds on the branches,
And roses flutter up.

I'm always looking for your lips
Behind a thousand kisses.

A night of gold,
Stars made of night . . .
Nobody sees us.

When the light comes up with the green
We're slumbering;
Only our shoulders play like butterflies.

EIN LIED DER LIEBE

Seit du nicht da bist,
Ist die Stadt dunkel.

Ich sammle die Schatten
Der Palmen auf,
Darunter du wandeltest.

Immer muß ich eine Melodie summen,
Die hängt lächelnd an den Ästen.

Du liebst mich wieder—
Wem soll ich mein Entzücken sagen?

Einer Waise oder einem Hochzeitler,
Der im Widerhall das Glück hört.

Ich weiß immer,
Wann du an mich denkst—

Dann wird mein Herz ein Kind
Und schreit.

An jedem Tor der Straße
Verweile ich und träume;

Ich helfe der Sonne deine Schönheit malen
An allen Wänden der Häuser.

Aber ich magere
An deinem Bilde.

Um schlanke Säulen schlinge ich mich
Bis sie schwanken.

Überall steht Wildedel,
Die Blüten unseres Blutes.

Wir tauchen in heilige Moose,
Die aus der Wolle goldener Lämmer sind.

Wenn doch ein Tiger
Seinen Leib streckte

A SONG OF LOVE

Since you have been gone
The city is dark.

I pick up the shadows
Of the palms
By which you wandered.

I always have to hum a melody;
It hangs there, smiling, in the branches.

You love me again—
To whom shall I tell my rapture?

To an orphan girl or a bridegroom
Who, in the echo, hears happiness.

I always know
When you think of me.

Then my heart becomes a child
And cries.

At every gate of the street
I stop and dream.

I help the sun to paint your beauty
On all the walls of the houses.

But I grow lean
On your image.

I twine myself around slender pillars
Until they sway.

Everywhere stands noblewild,
The blossoms of our blood.

We plunge into holy mosses
Which are made of the wool of golden lambs.

If only a tiger
Would stretch his body

Über die Ferne, die uns trennt,
Wie zu einem nahen Stern.

Auf meinem Angesicht
Liegt früh dein Hauch.

SASCHA

Um deine Lippen blüht noch jung
Der Trotz dunkelrot,

Aber auf deiner Stirne sind meine Gebete
Vom Sturm verwittert.

Daß wir uns im Leben
Nie küssen sollten . . .

Nun bist du der Engel,
Der auf meinem Grab steht.

Das Atmen der Erde bewegt
Meinen Leib wie lebendig.

Mein Herz scheint hell
Vom Rosenblut der Hecken.

Aber ich bin tot, Sascha,
Und das Lächeln liegt abgepflückt
Nur noch kurz auf meinem Gesicht.

Over the distance that divides us,
Like to a near star.

Upon my countenance
You breathe betimes.

SASCHA

Young defiance blooms yet
Dark red around your lips.

On your brow my prayers are
Beaten by the storm.

Strange that we never kissed
Our whole life long . . .

Now you are the angel
Who's standing on my grave.

The earth's breath stirs
My body, as if alive.

My heart shines bright
From the rose blood of the hedge.

But, Sascha, I am dead,
And my smile has been plucked off
And lies just a brief time still upon my face.

SENNA HOY

Seit du begraben liegst auf dem Hügel,
Ist die Erde süß.

Wo ich hingehe nun auf Zehen,
Wandele ich über reine Wege.

O deines Blutes Rosen
Durchtränken sanft den Tod.

Ich habe keine Furcht mehr
Vor dem Sterben.

Auf deinem Grabe blühe ich schon
Mit den Blumen der Schlingpflanzen.

Deine Lippen haben mich immer gerufen,
Nun weiß mein Name nicht mehr zurück.

Jede Schaufel Erde, die dich barg,
Verschüttete auch mich.

Darum ist immer Nacht an mir,
Und Sterne schon in der Dämmerung.

Und ich bin unbegreiflich unseren Freunden
Und ganz fremd geworden.

Aber du stehst am Tor der stillsten Stadt
Und wartest auf mich, du Großengel.

SENNA HOY

Since you've been lying buried on the hill
The earth is sweet.

Wherever I go on tiptoe now
I wander immaculate ways.

Oh the roses of your blood
Softly drench death through.

No longer do I feel
The fear of dying.

Upon your grave I bloom
With the flowers of vines.

Your lips called to me always,
Now my name finds no way back.

Every shovel of earth that hid you
Buried me also.

Therefore night is in me always,
And stars already in the twilight.

And I am incomprehensible to our friends
And become a stranger.

But you stand at the gate of the stillest city,
And wait for me, Great Angel.

HANS EHRENBAUM-DEGELE

Er war der Ritter in Goldrüstung.
Sein Herz ging auf sieben Rubinen.

Darum trugen seine Tage
Den lauteren Sonntagsglanz.

Sein Leben war ein lyrisches Gedicht,
Die Kriegsballade sein Tod.

Er sang den Frauen Lieder
In süßerlei Abendfarben.

Goldnelken waren seine Augen,
Manchmal stand Tau in ihnen.

Einmal sagte er zu mir:
»Ich muß früh sterben.«

Da weinten wir beide
Wie nach seinem Begräbnis.

Seitdem lagen seine Hände
Oft in den meinen.

Immer hab ich sie gestreichelt,
Bis sie die Waffe ergriffen.

HANS EHRENBAUM-DEGELE

He was the knight in gold armor.
His heart ran on seven rubies.

That's why his days conveyed
The perfect Sunday splendor.

His life was a lyric poem,
The ballad of war his death.

Songs he sang to the women
In sweet kinds of evening colors.

And gold carnations were his eyes,
Sometimes with dew upon them.

One day he told me:
"I'll surely die young."

Then we both wept together
As if at his funeral.

Ever since that his hands
Lay often in mine.

I always caressed them
Till they reached for the gun.

AN DEN RITTER AUS GOLD

Du bist alles was aus Gold ist
In der großen Welt.

Ich suche deine Sterne
Und will nicht schlafen.

Wir wollen uns hinter Hecken legen,
Uns niemehr aufrichten.

Aus unseren Händen
Süße Träumerei küssen.

Mein Herz holt sich
Von deinem Munde Rosen.

Meine Augen lieben dich an,
Du haschst nach ihren Faltern.

Was soll ich tun,
Wenn du nicht da bist.

Von meinen Lidern
Tropft schwarzer Schnee;

Wenn ich tot bin,
Spiele du mit meiner Seele.

TO THE KNIGHT OF GOLD

You are everything that is gold
In the great world.

I seek your stars
And have no wish to sleep.

Let us lie down behind hedges,
Never rise up again.

Out of our hands
Let's kiss sweet reveries.

My heart fetches
Roses from your mouth.

My eyes look love at you;
You snatch at their butterflies.

What shall I do
When you're not here.

From my lids
Drips black snow.

When I am dead:
Please play with my soul.

O, DEINE HÄNDE

Sind meine Kinder.
Alle meine Spielsachen
Liegen in ihren Gruben.

Immer spiel ich Soldaten
Mit deinen Fingern, kleine Reiter,
Bis sie umfallen.

Wie ich sie liebe
Deine Bubenhände, die zwei.

OH, YOUR HANDS

Are my children.
All of my playthings
Lie in their hollows.

I always play soldiers
With your fingers, little riders,
Till they fall down.

How I do love them,
The two of them, your boy's hands.

GISELHEER DEM HEIDEN

Ich weine—
Meine Träume fallen in die Welt.

In meine Dunkelheit
Wagt sich kein Hirte.

Meine Augen zeigen nicht den Weg
Wie die Sterne.

Immer bettle ich vor deiner Seele;
Weißt du das?

Wär ich doch blind—
Dächte dann, ich läg in deinem Leib.

Alle Blüten täte ich
Zu deinem Blut.

Ich bin vielreich,
Niemandwer kann mich pflücken;

Oder meine Gaben tragen
Heim.

Ich will dich ganz zart mich lehren;
Schon weißt du mich zu nennen.

Sieh meine Farben,
Schwarz und stern

Und mag den kühlen Tag nicht,
Der hat ein Glasauge.

Alles ist tot,
Nur du und ich nicht.

TO GISELHEER THE HEATHEN

I weep—
My dreams fall into the world.

Into my darkness
No shepherd dares to come.

My eyes do not point the way
Like stars.

I'm always begging from your soul;
Are you aware?

Were I only blind—
I'd think I was lying in your body.

All blossoms would I add
Unto your blood.

I am muchly rich;
No anybody can pluck me;

Or carry my gifts
Home.

I'll teach me to you quite gently;
Already you know what I'm called.

Look at my colors,
Black and star.

And I don't like the cool day;
It has a glass eye.

Everything's dead
Except you and me.

LAUTER DIAMANT

Ich hab in deinem Antlitz
Meinen Sternenhimmel ausgeträumt.

Alle meine bunten Kosenamen
Gab ich dir,

Und legte die Hand
Unter deinen Schritt,

Als ob ich dafür
Ins Jenseits käme.

Immer weint nun
Vom Himmel deine Mutter,

Da ich mich schnitzte
Aus deinem Herzfleische,

Und du so viel Liebe
Launisch verstießest.

Dunkel ist es—
Es flackert nur noch
Das Licht meiner Seele.

PURE DIAMOND

I've finished dreaming in your face
About my starry sky.

All of my colorful pet names
I gave to you.

And laid my hand
Beneath your foot

As if for that
I'd get to Heaven.

Now from Beyond
Your mother is weeping still,

Since I carved myself
From your heart's flesh,

And peevishly
You turned down so much love.

It's dark—
The only flickering still
Is the light of my soul.

DAS LIED DES SPIELPRINZEN

Wie kann ich dich mehr noch lieben?
Ich sehe den Tieren und Blumen
Bei der Liebe zu.

Küssen sich zwei Sterne,
Oder bilden Wolken ein Bild—
Wir spielten es schon zarter.

Und deine harte Stirne,
Ich kann mich so recht an sie lehnen,
Sitz drauf wie auf einem Giebel.

Und in deines Kinnes Grube
Bau ich mir ein Raubnest—
Bis—du mich aufgefressen hast.

Find dann einmal morgens
Nur noch meine Kniee,
Zwei gelbe Skarabäen für eines Kaisers Ring.

THE SONG OF THE PLAYMATE PRINCE

How can I love you even more?
I watch the flowers and animals
At their love.

If two stars kiss,
Or if clouds form a picture—
We've already played it more gently still.

And your hard brow,
I can really lean myself against it,
Sit on it like on a gable.

And in the hollow of your chin
I build a robber's hideaway—
Until—you've eaten me all up.

Find then one fine morning
Only my knees left over,
Two yellow scarabs for an emperor's ring.

HINTER BÄUMEN BERG ICH MICH

Bis meine Augen ausgeregnet haben,

Und halte sie tief verschlossen,
Daß niemand dein Bild schaut.

Ich schlang meine Arme um dich
Wie Gerank.

Bin doch mit dir verwachsen,
Warum reißt du mich von dir?

Ich schenkte dir die Blüte
Meines Leibes,

Alle meine Schmetterlinge
Scheuchte ich in deinen Garten.

Immer ging ich durch Granaten.
Sah durch dein Blut

Die Welt überall brennen
Vor Liebe.

Nun aber schlage ich mit meiner Stirn
Meine Tempelwände düster.

O du falscher Gaukler,
Du spanntest ein loses Seil.

Wie kalt mir alle Grüße sind,
Mein Herz liegt bloß,

Mein rot Fahrzeug
Pocht grausig.

Bin immer auf See
Und lande nicht mehr.

I HIDE BEHIND TREES

Until my eyes are rained out dry,

And keep them locked up tight
So nobody sees your picture.

I twisted my arms around you
Like long vines.

I'm grown to you after all;
Why do you tear me from you?

I gave you the budding
Of my body;

Shooed all my butterflies
Into your garden.

I walked and walked through the pomegranate trees,
Saw through your blood

The world burning everywhere
From love.

But now with my brow I beat
Dismally the walls of my temples.

O you false trickster,
You strung a loose rope.

How cold all greetings seem to me;
My heart lies bare.

My red vehicle
Knocks dreadfully.

I am always at sea
And land no longer.

GISELHEER DEM TIGER

Über dein Gesicht schleichen die Dschungeln.
O, wie du bist!

Deine Tigeraugen sind süß geworden
In der Sonne.

Ich trag dich immer herum
Zwischen meinen Zähnen.

Du mein Indianerbuch,
Wild West,
Siouxhäuptling!

Im Zwielicht schmachte ich
Gebunden am Buxbaumstamm—

Ich kann nicht mehr sein
Ohne das Skalpspiel.

Rote Küsse malen deine Messer
Auf meine Brust—

Bis mein Haar an deinem Gürtel flattert.

TO GISELHEER THE TIGER

The jungles creep across your face.
Oh, how you are!

Your tiger's eyes have sweetened
In the sun.

I'm carrying you around
Between my teeth.

You, my Indian book,
Wild West,
Sioux chief!

I languish in the twilight
Lashed to a boxwood tree—

I can't get along any more
Without the scalp game.

Your knives draw red kisses
On my breast—

Until my hair is fluttering on your belt.

O GOTT

Überall nur kurzer Schlaf
Im Mensch, im Grün, im Kelch der Winde.
Jeder kehrt in sein totes Herz heim.

—Ich wollt die Welt wär noch ein Kind—
Und wüßte mir vom ersten Atem zu erzählen.

Früher war eine große Frömmigkeit am Himmel,
Gaben sich die Sterne die Bibel zu lesen.
Könnte ich einmal Gottes Hand fassen
Oder den Mond an seinem Finger sehn.

O Gott, o Gott, wie weit bin ich von dir!

HÖRE

Ich raube in den Nächten
Die Rosen deines Mundes,
Daß keine Weibin Trinken findet.

Die dich umarmt,
Stiehlt mir von meinen Schauern,
Die ich um deine Glieder malte.

Ich bin dein Wegrand.
Die dich streift,
Stürzt ab.

Fühlst du mein Lebtum
Überall
Wie ferner Saum?

O GOD

Only a brief sleep everywhere
In man, in the green, in the cup of the winds.
Everyone goes home to his dead heart.

—I wish the world were still a child—
And was able to tell me how it first drew breath.

One time there was great piety in heaven;
The stars passed the Bible around to read.
If only I could take God's hand sometime
Or see on his finger the spinning moon.

O God, O God, how far I am from you!

LISTEN

I steal at night
The roses of your mouth,
So no she-woman will find drink.

She that hugs you
Robs me of my shuddering
Which I painted around your limbs.

I am your road's edge.
She that skirts you
Plunges down.

Do you feel my lifedom
Everywhere
Like a distant rim?

VERINNERLICHT

Ich denke immer ans Sterben,
Mich hat niemand lieb.

Ich wollt ich wär still Heiligenbild
Und alles in mir ausgelöscht.

Träumerisch färbte Abendrot
Meine Augen wund verweint.

Weiß nicht wo ich hin soll
Wie überall zu dir.

Bist meine heimliche Heimat
Und will nichts Leiseres mehr.

Wie blühte ich gern süß empor
An deinem Herzen himmelblau—

Lauter weiche Wege
Legte ich um dein pochend Haus.

TURNED INWARD

I think of dying all the time;
Nobody loves me.

I wish I were a quiet icon
And everything extinguished in me.

The dreamy sundown red would dye
My eyes all sore from crying.

I don't know where to turn to,
Except everywhere to you.

You're my secret homeland,
And I want nothing quieter.

How glad I'd be to sweetly flower
Up around your sky-blue heart—

Many a soft path I laid
About your throbbing house.

NUR DICH

Der Himmel trägt im Wolkengürtel
Den gebogenen Mond.

Unter dem Sichelbild
Will ich in deiner Hand ruhn.

Immer muß ich wie der Sturm will,
Bin ein Meer ohne Strand.

Aber seit du meine Muscheln suchst,
Leuchtet mein Herz.

Das liegt auf meinem Grund
Verzaubert.

Vielleicht ist mein Herz die Welt,
Pocht—

Und sucht nur noch dich—
Wie soll ich dich rufen?

ONLY FOR YOU

The sky wears in a belt of clouds
The bended moon.

Under the sickle image
I want to rest within your hand.

I always have to do the will of the storm;
Am a sea without shore.

But since you seek my seashells
My heart glows.

It lies at the bottom of me
Under a spell.

Perhaps my heart is the world,
Beats—

And searches only for you—
How should I call you?

DEM BARBAREN

Deine rauhen Blutstropfen
Süßen auf meiner Haut.

Nenne meine Augen nicht Verräterinnen,
Da sie deine Himmel umschweben;

Ich lehne lächelnd an deiner Nacht
Und lehre deine Sterne spielen.

Und trete singend durch das rostige Tor
Deiner Seligkeit.

Ich liebe dich und nahe weiß
Und verklärt auf Wallfahrtzehen.

Trage dein hochmütiges Herz,
Den reinen Kelch den Engeln entgegen.

Ich liebe dich wie nach dem Tode
Und meine Seele liegt über dich gebreitet—

Meine Seele fing alle Leiden auf,
Dich erschüttern ihre schmerzlichen Bilder.

Aber so viele Rosen blühen,
Die ich dir schenken will;

O, ich möchte dir alle Gärten bringen
In einem Kranz.

Immer denke ich an dich,
Bis die Wolken sinken;

Wir wollen uns küssen—
Nicht?

TO THE BARBARIAN

Your blood's rough drops
Are sweetening on my flesh.

Don't call my eyes traitoresses,
Since they float around your skies.

Smiling I lean upon your night
And teach your stars to play.

And enter singing the rusty gate
Of your blissfulness.

I love you and come near
White and transfigured on pilgrim's toes.

Carry your proud heart,
Pure chalice, towards the angels.

I love you as after death
And my soul lies spread upon you—

My soul caught up all sorrows;
You're shaken by its painful images.

But so many roses flower
That I want to give you;

Oh, I'd like to bring you all my gardens
In one wreath.

Always I think of you
Till the clouds descend;

Let's kiss each other—
Yes?

DEM BARBAREN

Ich liege in den Nächten
Auf deinem Angesicht.

Auf deines Leibes Steppe
Pflanze ich Zedern und Mandelbäume.

Ich wühle in deiner Brust unermüdlich
Nach den goldenen Freuden Pharaos.

Aber deine Lippen sind schwer,
Meine Wunder erlösen sie nicht.

Hebe doch deine Schneehimmel
Von meiner Seele—

Deine diamantnen Träume
Schneiden meine Adern auf.

Ich bin Joseph und trage einen süßen Gürtel
Um meine bunte Haut.

Dich beglückt das erschrockene Rauschen
Meiner Muscheln.

Aber dein Herz läßt keine Meere mehr ein.
O du!

TO THE BARBARIAN

I lie in the nights
Upon your countenance,

On the steppes of your body
Plant cedars and almond trees.

Ceaselessly I rummage in your breast
For the Pharaoh's golden joys.

But your lips are hard;
My miracles don't redeem them.

Please lift your snow-filled skies
From off my soul—

Your diamond dreams
Cut open my arteries.

I am Joseph and wear a sweet girdle
About my bright skin.

My seashells' frightened roar
Enraptures you.

But your heart lets no more oceans in.
O you!

DEM HERZOG VON LEIPZIG

Deine Augen sind gestorben;
Du warst so lange auf dem Meer.

Aber auch ich bin
Ohne Strand.

Meine Stirne ist aus Muschel.
Tang und Seestern hängen an mir.

Einmal möchte ich mit meiner ziellosen Hand
Über dein Gesicht fassen,

Oder eine Eidechse über deine Lippen
Liebentlang mich kräuseln.

Weihrauch strömt aus deiner Haut,
Und ich will dich feiern,

Dir bringen meine Gärten,
Überall blüht mein Herz bunt auf.

TO THE DUKE OF LEIPZIG

Your eyes have died;
You were so long at sea.

But I too am
Without a beach.

My forehead is made of mussel shell.
Sea-tang and starfish are hanging on me.

I'd like sometime with an aimless hand
To feel across your face,

Or, a lizard across your lips,
Curl myself love-along.

Incense rises from your skin,
And I would celebrate you,

Bring to you my gardens;
My heart opens everywhere in bright bloom.

ABER DEINE BRAUEN SIND UNWETTER

In der Nacht schweb ich ruhlos am Himmel
Und werde nicht dunkel vom Schlaf.

Um mein Herz schwirren Träume
Und wollen Süßigkeit.

Ich habe lauter Zacken an den Randen,
Nur du trinkst Gold unversehrt.

Ich bin ein Stern
In der blauen Wolke deines Angesichts.

Wenn mein Glanz in deinem Auge spielt,
Sind wir eine Welt.

Und würden entschlummern verzückt—
Aber deine Brauen sind Unwetter.

DU MACHST MICH TRAURIG—HÖR

Bin so müde.
Alle Nächte trag ich auf dem Rücken
Auch deine Nacht,
Die du so schwer umträumst.

Hast du mich lieb?
Ich blies dir arge Wolken von der Stirn
Und tat ihr blau.

Was tust du mir in meiner Todesstunde?

BUT YOUR BROWS ARE A STORM

At night I hover restless in the heavens
And don't become dark with sleep.

Dreams whir around my heart
Desiring sweetness.

I am covered with sharp points along the edges;
You alone drink gold unharmed.

I am a star
In the blue cloud of your face.

When in your eye my splendor plays
We are one world.

And would fall into rapturous slumber—
But your brows are a storm.

YOU MAKE ME SAD—LISTEN

Am so tired.
I carry all the nights upon my back
Your night too,
That you wrap in such thick dreams.

Do you love me?
I blew some wicked clouds off of your brow
And made it blue.

What will you do for me in my hour of death?

DEM KÖNIG VON BÖHMEN

Ich frage nicht mehr—
Ich weiß wer auf den Sternen wohnt.

Mein Herz sinkt tief in die Nacht.
So sterben Liebende
Immer an zärtlichen Himmeln vorbei;

Und atmen wieder dem Morgen entgegen
Auf frühleisen Schweben.
Ich aber wandele mit den heimkehrenden Sternen.

Und ich habe viele schlafende Knospen ausgelöscht,
Will ihr Sterben nicht sehn,
Wenn die Rosenhimmel tanzen.

Aus dem Gold meiner Stirne leuchtet der Smaragd,
Der den Sommer färbt.
Ich bin eine Prinzessin.

Mein Herz sinkt tief in die Nacht
An Liebende vorbei.

TO THE KING OF BOHEMIA

I no longer ask—
I know who lives on the stars.

My heart sinks deep into the night.
Thus lovers die
On and on past gentle heavens.

And breathe again towards the morning
On softly early wings.
But I am wandering with the homeward stars.

And I have extinguished many sleeping buds;
Don't want to see their dying
When the rosy heavens dance.

From the gold of my brow the emerald gleams
That tints the summer.
I am a princess.

My heart sinks deep into the night
On past the lovers.

DEM DANIEL JESUS PAUL

Du es ist Nacht—
Wir wollen unsere Sehnsucht teilen,
Und in die Goldgebilde blicken.

Vor meinem Herzen sitzt immer eine Tote
Und bettelt um Almosen.

Und summt meine Lieder
Schon einen weißgewordenen Sommer lang.

Über den Grabweg hinweg
Wollen wir uns lieben,

Tollkühne Knaben,
Könige, die sich nur mit dem Szepter berühren!

Frage nicht—ich lausche
Deiner Augen Rauschehonig.

Die Nacht ist eine weiche Rose,
Wir wollen uns in ihren Kelch legen,

Immer ferner versinken,
Ich bin müde vom Tod!

TO DANIEL JESUS PAUL

Look, it is night—
Let us share our longing
And gaze into the shapes of gold.

A dead woman's always sitting by my heart
Begging for alms.

And hums my songs
The whole white summer long.

Let us love one another
Across the grave path and beyond,

Bold, brash boys,
Kings, who touch one another with scepters only.

Don't ask—I'm listening
To the drunken honey of your eyes.

The night is a soft rose;
Let us lie down in its cup,

Sink further and further;
I am tired of death!

ABSCHIED

Aber du kamst nie mit dem Abend—
Ich saß im Sternenmantel.

. . . Wenn es an mein Haus pochte,
War es mein eigenes Herz.

Das hängt nun an jedem Türpfosten,
Auch an deiner Tür;

Zwischen Farren verlöschende Feuerrose
Im Braun der Guirlande.

Ich färbte dir den Himmel brombeer
Mit meinem Herzblut.

Aber du kamst nie mit dem Abend—
. . . Ich stand in goldenen Schuhen.

LEAVE-TAKING

But you never came with the evening—
I sat in a robe of stars.

　. . When there was a knock at the door
It was only my own heart.

This hangs now on every doorpost,
On your door too.

Between ferns, expiring fire-roses
In the brown of the garland.

I colored the heavens blackberry for you
With my heart's blood.

But you never came with the evening—
. . . I stood there in golden shoes.

SAVARY LE DUC

Wie Perlen hängen seine Bilder
Schaumleicht an seidenen Wänden aufgereiht.

Mit goldenem Harz der Hagebutten
Und Rosenseime,
Malt er der Prinzen Liebeskleid.

Um ihren zarten Schultern tragen sie
An Ketten—Souvenir—im Medaillon
Verzückt des Freundes Paradeis.

Und ihre Hände spielen mit den Bächen
Und feinen Blumenstengeln
Und dem jungen Reis.

Und necken gern den Ziegenbock.
Glasäugig lauscht die graue Geiß.

Und ihre Leiber lieben sich
Wie süßgeblühte Bohnenstöcke,
Die sich bewegen kaum in ihrer Adeligkeit.

SAVARY LE DUC

His pictures hang like pearls
As light as foam, in rows on silken walls.

With golden resin of haws
And honey of rose
He paints the love-dress of the princes.

Around their delicate shoulders they are wearing
On chains—a souvenir—inside a locket,
Rapturously, their friend's paradise.

And their hands play with the streams
And the fine stems of flowers
And the young branch.

And like to tease the bearded goat.
Glassy-eyed the she-goat listens.

And their bodies love each other
Like bean poles in sweet bloom
That hardly move in their gentility.

UNSER LIEBESLIED

Unter der Wehmut der Esche
Lächeln die Augen meiner Freundin.

Und ich muß weinen
Überall wo Rosen aufblühn.

Wir hören beide unseren Namen nicht—
Immer Nachtwandlerinnen zwischen den bunten Jünglingen.

Meine Freundin gaukelt mit dem Mond,
Unserm Sternenspiel folgen Erschrockene nach.

O, unsere Schwärmerei berauscht
Die Straßen und Plätze der Stadt.

Alle Träume lauschen gebannt hinter den Hecken
Kann nicht Morgen werden—

Und die seidige Nacht uns beiden
Tausendmalimmer um den Hals geschlungen.

Wie ich mich drehen muß!

Und meine Freundin küßt taumelnd den Rosigtau
Unter dem Düster des Trauerbaums.

OUR LOVE SONG

Under the sadness of the ash tree
Smile the eyes of her my friend.

And I must cry
Everywhere where roses bloom.

Both of us do not hear our name—
Sleepwalkers always in the night among the colorful young men.

My friend is juggling with the moon,
Our game of stars is followed by startled people.

Oh, our mad fantasies intoxicate
The streets and squares of the city.

All the dreams listen spellbound behind the hedges
The morning cannot dawn—

And the silken night is wound
A thousand-times-always around our necks.

How I must whirl about!

And my friend kisses reeling the rosy dew
Under the gloomy of the mourning tree.

ABDUL ANTINOUS

Deine Schlankheit fließt wie dunkles Geschmeide.
O du meine wilde Mitternachtssonne,
Küsse mein Herz, meine rotpochende Erde.

Wie groß aufgetan deine Augen sind—
Du hast den Himmel gesehn
So nah, so tief.

Und ich habe auf deiner Schulter
Mein Land gebaut—
Wo bist du?

Zögernd wie dein Fuß ist der Weg—
Sterne werden meine Blutstropfen. . . .
Du, ich liebe dich, ich liebe dich.

ABDUL ANTINOUS

Your slimness flows like a dark jewelry.
O you, my savage midnight sun;
Kiss my heart, my own red-throbbing earth.

How wide your eyes stand open—
You have seen the sky
So near, so deep.

And I have built my land
Upon your shoulder—
Where are you?

Like your foot, the path is hesitant—
The drops of my blood become stars. . . .
You, I love you, I love you.

PABLO

Pablo nachts höre ich die Palmenblätter
Unter deinen Füßen rascheln.

Manchmal muß ich sehr weinen
Um dich vor Glück—

Dann wächst ein Lächeln
Auf deinem lässigen Lide.

Oder es geht dir eine seltene Freude auf:
Deines Herzens schwarze Aster.

Immer wenn du an Gärten vorbei
Das Ende deines Weges erblickst, Pablo,

—Es ist mein ewiger Liebesgedanke,
Der zu dir will.

Und oft wird Schimmer vom Himmel fallen,
Denn es sucht dich am Abend mein goldener Seufzer.

Bald kommt der schmachtende Monat
Über deine holde Stadt;

Unter dem Gartenbaum hängen
Wie bunte Trauben die Vögelscharen,

Und auch ich warte verzaubert
Von Traum behangen.

Du stolzer Eingeborener, Pablo,
Von deinem Angesicht atme ich fremde Liebeslaute;

In deiner Schläfe aber will ich meinen Glücksstern pflanzen,
Mich berauben meiner leuchtenden Blüte.

PABLO

Pablo at night I hear the palm leaves
Rustle beneath your feet.

Sometimes I have to cry a lot
From happiness about you.

Then a smile grows
On your hooded eyelids.

Or a rare joy opens for you:
Your heart's black aster.

Whenever past the gardens
You see the end of your pathway, Pablo,

—It's my eternal thought of love
Desiring to join you.

And often a glow will fall from heaven,
For in the evening my golden sigh goes searching for you.

Soon the languishing month arrives
Over your dear city;

Under the garden tree there hang
Flocks of birds like gaily colored grapes.

And I too wait enchanted
Hung about by dream.

You proud native, Pablo,
I breathe from your countenance strange sounds of love;

But on your brow I want to plant my fortunate star,
Rob myself of my luminous blossom.

ABSCHIED

Ich wollte dir immerzu
Viele Liebesworte sagen,

Nun suchst du ruhlos
Nach verlorenen Wundern.

Aber wenn meine Spieluhren spielen
Feiern wir Hochzeit.

O, deine süßen Augen
Sind meine Lieblingsblumen.

Und dein Herz ist mein Himmelreich. . . .
Laß mich hineinschaun.

Du bist ganz aus glitzernder Minze
Und so weich versonnen.

Ich wollte dir immerzu
Viele Liebesworte sagen,

Warum tat ich das nicht?

LEAVE-TAKING

Over and over I wanted to
Say to you many words of love.

You search now restlessly
After lost miracles.

But when my music boxes play
We'll hold our wedding.

Oh, your sweet eyes
Are my favorite flowers.

And your heart is my kingdom of heaven. . . .
Let me peer into it.

You are all of glittering mint
And so softly dreamy.

Over and over I wanted to
Say to you many words of love;

Why didn't I do it?

DER MÖNCH

In deinem Blick schweben
Alle Himmel zusammen.

Immer hast du die Madonna angesehn,
Darum sind deine Augen überirdisch.

Und mein Herz wird ein Weihbecken,
Besterne dich mit meinem Blut;

Ich will der Tau deiner Frühe sein,
Deiner Abendsehnsucht pochendes Amen.

Du bist heilig zwischen bösem Tanz
Und schrillen Flöten.

Gottes Nachtigall bist du
In seinem Hirtentraum.

Deine Sünden wurden Musik,
Die bewegt süß meine Züge;

Deine Tränen tranken schlafende Blumen,
Die wieder Paradies werden sollen.

Ich liebe dich zauberisch wie im Spiegel des Bachs
Oder fern im wolkengerahmten Blau.

THE MONK

In your glance all the heavens
Float together.

You were always watching the Madonna;
That's why your eyes are so unearthly.

And my heart becomes a holy font;
Bestar yourself here with my blood.

I want to be the dew of your youth,
The pulsing amen of your evening's longing.

You are holy, between evil dance
And shrilling flutes.

God's nightingale you are
In His shepherd's dream.

Your sins became music;
It sweetly moves my features;

Your dreams drank sleeping flowers
Which were to be paradise again.

I love you magically, as in the mirror of the stream,
Or far in the cloud-framed blue.

DEM MÖNCH

Ich taste überall nach deinem Schein.
Suchst du mich auch?

In meiner Stirne leuchtet
Der erblaßte Stern wieder,

Und sehe dich nur in der Welt,
Dein Lächeln immerfort.

Unsere himmelweißen Herzen
Erglühen im Schlaf.

O wir möchten uns küssen,
Aber es wäre wie Mord.

Ich stehe ganz bunt am Granatbaum
In einem Bilderbuch.

Manchmal schaust du auf mich—
Dann singen die Junivögel.

TO THE MONK

Everywhere I grope for your bright seeming.
Do you seek me too?

On my forehead gleams
Once more the faded star,

And I see you only in the world,
Your smile forever.

Our sky-white hearts
Begin to glow in sleep.

Oh we'd like to kiss
But it would be like murder.

I stand quite colorfully at the pomegranate tree
In a picture book.

Sometimes you look at me—
Then the June birds sing.

DEM MÖNCH

Meine Zehen wurden Knospen.
—Sieh, so komm ich zu dir.

Du bist am Rand über dem Tal
Die leuchtende Großkornblume;

Mit deinem Glück färbt sich
Der Himmel die Wangen blau.

Immer öffnet sich mein Wesen—
—Bin eine glitzernde Nische,

Aber du kommst nie zu deiner Anbetung,
Und morgen ist ewige Nacht.

Meine Sehnsucht ist im Sturm meiner Augen
Lange schon verwittert,

Die Korallen in meinem Blut
Sind ganz erblaßt.

Zwischen Dunkelheit verlischt mein Leben
Im scheidenden Antlitz des Mondes.

TO THE MONK

My toes became flower buds.
—See, thus I come to you.

At the rim of the valley you are
The luminous great cornflower.

Heaven dyes its cheeks
Blue with your happiness.

My being always opens—
—I'm a glittering niche,

But you never come to your worship
And tomorrow is endless night.

My longing has, in the storm of my eyes,
Long ago weathered away.

The corals in my blood
Are gone quite pale.

Between darkness my life is extinguished
In the departing countenance of the moon.

EIN LIED

Hinter meinen Augen stehen Wasser,
Die muß ich alle weinen.

Immer möcht ich auffliegen,
Mit den Zugvögeln fort;

Buntatmen mit den Winden
In der großen Luft.

O ich bin so traurig – – – –
Das Gesicht im Mond weiß es.

Drum ist viel samtne Andacht
Und nahender Frühmorgen um mich.

Als an deinem steinernen Herzen
Meine Flügel brachen,

Fielen die Amseln wie Trauerrosen
Hoch vom blauen Gebüsch.

Alles verhaltene Gezwitscher
Will wieder jubeln,

Und ich möchte auffliegen
Mit den Zugvögeln fort.

A SONG

Behind my eyes stand the waters;
I have to weep them all.

Always I'd like to take flight
With the birds moving on.

Bright breathe with the winds
In the vast air.

Oh I am so sad – – – –
The face in the moon well knows.

That's why much velvet devotion
And approaching morn surround me.

When on your stony heart
My wings were broken,

Blackbirds fell like funeral roses
Out of the high blue bush.

All of the long restrained twitter
Wants to rejoice again,

And I would like to take flight
With the birds moving on.

HEIMLICH ZUR NACHT

Ich habe dich gewählt
Unter allen Sternen.

Und bin wach—eine lauschende Blume
Im summenden Laub.

Unsere Lippen wollen Honig bereiten,
Unsere schimmernden Nächte sind aufgeblüht.

An dem seligen Glanz deines Leibes
Zündet mein Herz seine Himmel an—

Alle meine Träume hängen an deinem Golde,
Ich habe dich gewählt unter allen Sternen.

SECRETLY AT NIGHT

I have chosen you
Among all stars.

And am awake—a listening flower
In the hum of the leaves.

Our lips are eager to prepare their honey;
Our shimmering nights have blossomed forth.

On the blessed splendor of your body
My heart ignites its heavens.

All of my dreams hang from your gold;
I have chosen you among all stars.

FRANZ WERFEL

Ein entzückender Schuljunge ist er;
Lauter Lehrer spuken in seinem Lockenkopf.

Sein Name ist so mutwillig:
Franz Werfel.

Immer schreib ich ihm Briefe,
Die er mit Klecksen beantwortet.

Aber wir lieben ihn alle
Seines zarten, zärtlichen Herzens wegen.

Sein Herz hat Echo,
Pocht verwundert.

Und fromm werden seine Lippen
Im Gedicht.

Manches trägt einen staubigen Turban.
Er ist der Enkel seiner eigenen Verse.

Doch auf seiner Lippe
Ist eine Nachtigall gemalt.

Mein Garten singt,
Wenn er ihn verläßt.

Freude streut seine Stimme
Über den Weg.

FRANZ WERFEL

He's a delightful schoolboy,
Full of teachers that haunt his curly head.

His name is so roguish:
Franz Werfel.

The letters I always write him
He answers with inkblots.

But we all love him
Because of his delicate, tender heart.

His heart has an echo,
Beats astonished.

And his lips become pious
In his poems.

Much of it wears a dusty turban.
He's his own verses' grandson.

But on his lips
A nightingale is painted.

My garden sings
When he leaves it.

His voice strews joy
Upon the way.

PETER BAUM

Er war des Tannenbaums Urenkel,
Unter dem die Herren zu Elberfeld Gericht hielten.

Und freute sich an jedes glitzernd Wort
Und ließ sich feierlich plündern.

Dann leuchteten die beiden Saphire
In seinem fürstlichen Gesicht.

Immer drängte ich, wenn ich krank lag,
»Peter Baum soll kommen!!«

Kam er, war Weihnachten—
Ein Honigkuchen wurde dann mein Herz.

Wie konnten wir uns freuen!
Beide ganz egal.

Und oft bewachte er
Im Sessel schmausend meinen Schlummer.

Rote und gelbe Cyllaxbonbons aß er so gern;
Oft eine ganze Schüssel leer.

Nun schlummert unser lieber Pitter
Schon ewige Nächte lang.

»Wenn ich Euch alle glücklich erst
Im Himmel hätte—«

Sagte einmal gläubig zu den Söhnen
Seine Mutter.

Nun ist der Peter fern bewahrt
Im Himmel.

Und um des Dichters Riesenleib auf dem Soldatenkirchhof
Wächst sanft die Erde pietätvoll.

PETER BAUM

He was the fir tree's great-grandson
Under which the Lords of Elberfeld held court.

And took delight in every glittering word
And let himself be plundered festively.

Then both the sapphires glowed
In his princely face.

When I was sick, I always insisted:
"Have Peter Baum come over!!"

Whenever he came it was Christmas—
My heart turned to honey-cake then.

How jolly we were together!
Both of us just the same.

And often he guarded my slumber
Feasting in the easy chair.

He loved to eat red and yellow cyllax candies;
Sometimes emptied a whole bowl.

Now our dear Pete's been slumbering
These many endless nights.

"If only I already had you all
Happily in heaven—"

His mother once said devoutly
To her sons.

Now Peter is safely put away
In distant heaven.

And around the poet's vast body at the soldiers' cemetery
The earth grows soft and reverently.

GEORG TRAKL

Georg Trakl erlag im Krieg von eigener Hand gefällt.
So einsam war es in der Welt. Ich hatt ihn lieb.

GEORG TRAKL

Seine Augen standen ganz fern.
Er war als Knabe einmal schon im Himmel.

Darum kamen seine Worte hervor
Auf blauen und auf weißen Wolken.

Wir stritten über Religion,
Aber immer wie zwei Spielgefährten,

Und bereiteten Gott von Mund zu Mund.
Im Anfang war das Wort.

Des Dichters Herz, eine feste Burg,
Seine Gedichte: Singende Thesen.

Er war wohl Martin Luther.

Seine dreifaltige Seele trug er in der Hand,
Als er in den heiligen Krieg zog.

—Dann wußte ich, er war gestorben—

Sein Schatten weilte unbegreiflich
Auf dem Abend meines Zimmers.

GEORG TRAKL

Georg Trakl died in the war, cut down by his own hand.
So lonely was the world. I loved him.

GEORG TRAKL

His eyes stared far away.
Once as a boy he had already been in heaven.

That's why his words came forth
On clouds of blue and white.

We argued about religion,
But always like two playmates,

And prepared God from mouth to mouth.
In the beginning was the Word.

The poet's heart, a mighty fortress,
His poems: singing theses.

Probably he was Martin Luther.

His trinitarian soul he carried in his hand
When he went to the holy war.

—Then I knew he had died—

Incomprehensibly his shadow tarried
In the evening of my room.

ALICE TRÜBNER

Ihr Angesicht war aus Mondstein,
Darum mußte sie immer träumen.

Durch die Seide ihrer Ebenholzhaare
Schimmerte Tausendundeinenacht.

Ihre Augen weihsagten.
Ein goldenes Bibelblatt war ihr Herz.

Sie thronte einen Himmel hoch
Über die Freunde.

O sie war eine Sternin—
Schimmer streute sie von sich.

Eine Herzogin war sie
Und krönte den armseligsten Gast.

Manchmal aber kam sie vom West:
Ein Wetter in Blitzfarben;

Die sind gefangen über Burgzacken
Im harten Rahmen.

Ihre Bilder viele,
Pietätvolle, bunte Briefe;

Manche aufbewahrt unter Glas
An den Wänden.

Aber auch Gläser und Gräser
Malte Alice Trübner.

Irgendwo zwischen sitzt ein Schelm,
Ein altmodisch dicker Puppenporzellankopf.

Oder sie malte huldvoll die Köchin
Als Frau Lucullus gelassen im Lehnstuhl.

Verwandelte strotzende Früchte in Rosen
Auf weißem Damast.

O, sie war eine Zauberin.

ALICE TRÜBNER

Her face was made of moonstone;
That's why she was forever dreaming.

Through the silk of her ebony hair
A Thousand and One Nights came shimmering.

Her eyes spoke consecration.
Her heart was a golden Bible page.

Sky-high uprose her throne
Above her friends.

Oh she was a staress—
Strewed shimmering light around her.

A countess,
And crowned the most pitiful guest.

But sometimes she came from the West:
A lightning-colored storm;

It's caught above castle crags
In the hard frame.

Her many pictures,
Reverent, colorful letters;

Many preserved under glass
On the walls.

But Alice Trübner painted
Glasses and grasses also.

Somewhere among them sits a rogue,
A fat, old-fashioned head of a porcelain doll.

Or she graciously painted the cook
As Lady Lucullus relaxed in an easy chair.

Bursting fruit she transformed into roses
On white damask.

Oh, she was a sorceress.

GEORG GROSZ

Manchmal spielen bunte Tränen
In seinen äschernen Augen.

Aber immer begegnen ihm Totenwagen,
Die verscheuchen seine Libellen.

Er ist abergläubig—
—Ward unter einem großen Stern geboren—

Seine Schrift regnet,
Seine Zeichnung: Trüber Buchstabe.

Wie lange im Fluß gelegen,
Blähen seine Menschen sich auf.

Mysteriöse Verlorene mit Quappenmäulern
Und verfaulten Seelen.

Fünf träumende Totenfahrer
Sind seine silbernen Finger.

Aber nirgendwo ein Licht im verirrten Märchen
Und doch ist er ein Kind,

Der Held aus dem Lederstrumpf
Mit dem Indianerstamm auf Duzfuß.

Sonst haßt er alle Menschen,
Sie bringen ihm Unglück.

Aber Georg Grosz liebt sein Mißgeschick
Wie einen anhänglichen Feind.

Und seine Traurigkeit ist dionysisch,
Schwarzer Champagner seine Klage.

Er ist ein Meer mit verhängtem Mond,
Sein Gott ist nur scheintot.

GEORG GROSZ

Colorful tears will sometimes play
In his ashen eyes.

But he's always meeting funeral processions;
They chase away his dragonflies.

He's superstitious—
—Was born under a mighty star—

His handwriting rains;
His sketches: gloomy alphabet.

As if they'd lain a long time in the river,
His people puff and swell.

The mysterious lost, with tadpole maws
And rotten souls.

Five dreaming drivers of the dead
Are his silver fingers.

But nowhere a light in the fairy tale gone astray
And yet he is a child,

A hero like Leather Stocking
On familiar terms with the Indians.

Otherwise, he hates everybody;
They bring him bad luck.

But Georg Grosz loves his misfortune
Like an affectionate enemy.

And his sadness is Dionysian,
His plaint black champagne.

He is an ocean with clouded moon;
His God only seems to be dead.

HEINRICH MARIA DAVRINGHAUSEN

—Wie er daherkommt—
Trojanischer junger Priester
Auf grabaltem Holzgefäß.

Zwei Nachtschatten schlaftrinken
In seinem Mahagonikopf,
Seine Lippen küßte ein Gottmädchen hold.

—Wie er gefalten aufstrebt—
Immer tragen seine Schultern
Ehrfürchtigen Samt.

Seine Füße schreiten
Nur über gepflegte Wege,
Stolperten nie über Gestrüpp.

—Wie er gottverhalten ist—
Aus jedem Bild, das er malt,
Blickt allfarbig der Schöpfer.

HEINRICH MARIA DAVRINGHAUSEN

—How he comes walking—
Young Trojan priest
On a grave-old wooden vase.

Two night shadows sleep-drink
In his mahogany head;
A god-maiden kissed his lips sweet.

—How he strives upward, folded—
His shoulders wearing
Respectful velvet.

His feet go striding
Only on well-tended ways,
Never stumbled in underbrush.

—How god-reserved he is—
Out of each picture he paints
Peers the creator in every color.

MILLY STEGER

Milly Steger ist eine Bändigerin,
Haut Löwen und Panther in Stein.

Vor dem Spielhaus in Elberfeld
Stehen ihre Großgestalten;

Böse Tolpatsche, ernste Hännesken,
Clowne, die mit blutenden Seelen wehen.

Aber auch Brunnen, verschwiegene Weibsmopse
Zwingt Milly rätselhaft nieder.

Manchmal schnitzt die Gulliverin
Aus Zündhölzchen Adam und hinterrücks sein Weib.

Dann lacht sie wie ein Apfel;
Im stahlblauen Auge sitzt der Schalk.

Milly Steger ist eine Büffelin an Wurfkraft;
Freut sie sich auch an dem blühenden Kern der Büsche.

MILLY STEGER

Milly Steger is an animal tamer;
Chisels panthers and lions in stone.

Her monumental figures stand
In front of the Elberfeld Theater.

Wicked louts, dead-serious numbskulls,
Clowns that wave their bleeding souls.

But also fountains, discreet, plump females,
Milly mysteriously subjugates them.

Sometimes this lady Gulliver carves
Adam from matchsticks and—behind his back—his wife.

Then she laughs like an apple;
A rascally look in her steel-blue eye.

Milly Steger is a workhorse in full career;
The blooming root of the bushes makes her happy too.

LEO KESTENBERG

Seine Hände zaubern Musik durch stille Zimmer.
Zwischen uns sitzt dann der ehrwürdige Mond
Goldbehäbig im Lehnstuhl
Und versöhnt uns mit der Welt.

Wenn Leo Kestenberg Flügel spielt,
Ist er ein heiliger Mann;
Erweckt Liszt aus steinernem Schlaf,
Bach feiert Himmelfahrt.

Mit Schumann wird Leo ein Kind
Und Schwärmer am Süßfeuer Chopins.

Der dunkle Flügel verwandelt sich aber zur Orgel
Wenn Kestenberg eigene Rosen spielt.
Sein schweres Ebenholzherz frommütig aufhebt
Und weicher Musikregen uns durchrieselt.

LEO KESTENBERG

His hands can conjure music through still rooms.
Between us sits the reverend moon
Portly as gold in the armchair,
And reconciles us with the world

When Leo Kestenberg plays the grand piano
He is a holy man.
Wakens Liszt from stony sleep;
Bach celebrates ascension.

With Schumann Leo becomes a child
And a dreamer at the sweet fire of Chopin.

But the dark piano changes to an organ
When Kestenberg is playing his own roses.
His heavy ebony heart lifts piously
And through us trickles the soft music's rain.

LUDWIG HARDT

Seiner Heimat Erde ruht
An keiner Bergwand aus;

Ein weiter, weiter Schemel—
Friesland.

Ungehemmt wettern die Wetter
Und die stürmenden Gemüter dort.

Im lüttchen Städtchen Weener
Hockt Ludwigs zottigsteinern Elternnest.

Da einmal flog er mit den Herbstvögeln
Fort über die Ems.

Von hoher Vogelreinheit inbrünstig
Ohne Makel klopft sein Herz.

Und geharnischt ist seine Nase,
Seidene Spenderinnen die feinen Lippen,

Wenn sie die Verse Maria
Rainer Rilkes gastlich reichen.

Werden Rittersporn
In Liliencrons Balladengesängen;

Flattern wie Möven auf,
Lauter »Emmas«, wenn er entzückend

Uns mit Morgensterns
—frei nach Hardt—»kosmischer Meschuggas« beschenkt.

Oh, Ludwig Hardt liebt seine Dichter,
Die er spricht.

Und vermählt sich mit den Gedichten,
Die er schlicht zu sagen versteht.

Nie deklamiert er!
Das ist es eben.

LUDWIG HARDT

The earth of his homeland doesn't rest
On any mountain wall.

A wide, wide footstool—
Frisia.

The storms roar uninhibited there
And the stormy spirits too.

In the itty-bitty city of Weener
Squats Ludwig's shaggy stone parental nest.

From there he flew with the Autumn birds one day
Over the Ems and away.

Fervent with great bird-purity
His heart is immaculate.

And his nose is up in arms,
The fine lips are silken donoresses,

When they hospitably serve
Their verses of Maria Rainer Rilke.

They become larkspur, lance-like,
In the ballads of Liliencron;

Flutter like seagulls,
"Emmas" all, when with great charm

He honors us with Morgenstern's
"Cosmic meschuggas" (to paraphrase Hardt).

O Ludwig Hardt loves the poets
That he recites.

And marries the poems
That he can speak with such simplicity.

He never declaims!
That's just the point.

WILHELM SCHMIDTBONN

Er ist der Dichter, dem der Schlüssel
Zur Steinzeit vermacht wurde.

Adam den Urkäfer trägt er,
Ein Skarabäus im Ring.

Wilhelm Schmidtbonn erzählt vom Paradies;
Reißt den verlogenen Nebel vom Baum:
Stolz blüht die Dolde der Erkenntnis.

Sein markisches Gesicht strömt immer
Zwei dämmerblaue Kräfte aus.

Er ist aus Laub und Rinde,
Morgenfrühe und Kentauerblut.

Wie oft schon ließ er sich zur Ader
Seine Werke zu tränken.
Sein neustes Versspiel stiert aus Einauge.

WILHELM SCHMIDTBONN

He is the poet to whom was left
The key to the Stone Age.

He carries the old dawn-beetle Adam,
A scarab in his ring.

Wilhelm Schmidtbonn tells about Paradise;
Rips the hypocritical mist from the tree:
The flowers of knowledge blossom proudly.

His Prussian face beams out
Two dusk-blue forces.

He's made of leaf and bark,
Of early morn and centaur blood.

How often he has tapped his veins
To drench his work.
His newest verse-play stares out of one eye.

FRANZ MARC

Der blaue Reiter ist gefallen, ein Großbiblischer, an dem der Duft Edens hing. Über die Landschaft warf er einen blauen Schatten. Er war der, welcher die Tiere noch reden hörte; und er verklärte ihre unverstandenen Seelen. Immer erinnerte mich der blaue Reiter aus dem Kriege daran: es genügt nicht alleine, zu den Menschen gütig zu sein, und was du namentlich an den Pferden, da sie unbeschreiblich auf dem Schlachtfeld leiden müssen, Gutes tust, tust du mir.

Er ist gefallen. Seinen Riesenkörper tragen große Engel zu Gott, der hält seine blaue Seele, eine leuchtende Fahne, in seiner Hand. Ich denke an eine Geschichte im Talmud, die mir ein Priester erzählte: wie Gott mit den Menschen vor dem zerstörten Tempel stand und weinte. Denn wo der blaue Reiter ging, schenkte er Himmel. So viele Vögel fliegen durch die Nacht, sie können noch Wind und Atem spielen, aber wir wissen nichts mehr hier unten davon, wir können uns nur noch zerhacken oder gleichgültig aneinander vorbeigehen. In dieser Nüchternheit erhebt sich drohend eine unermeßliche Blutmühle, und wir Völker alle werden bald zermahlen sein. Schreiten immerfort über wartende Erde. Der blaue Reiter ist angelangt; er war noch zu jung zu sterben.

Nie sah ich irgendeinen Maler gotternster und sanfter malen wie ihn. »Zitronenochsen« und »Feuerbüffel« nannte er seine Tiere, und auf seiner Schläfe ging ein Stern auf. Aber auch die Tiere der Wildnis begannen pflanzlich zu werden in seiner tropischen Hand. Tigerinnen verzauberte er zu Anemonen, Leoparden legte er das Geschmeide der Levkoje um; er sprach vom *reinen* Totschlag, wenn auf seinem Bild sich der Panther die Gazell vom Fels holte. Er fühlte wie der junge Erzvater in der Bibelzeit, ein herrlicher Jakob er, der Fürst von Kana. Um seine Schultern schlug er wild das Dickicht; sein schönes Angesicht spiegelte er im Quell und sein Wunderherz trug er oftmals in Fell gehüllt, wie ein schlafendes Knäblein heim, über die Wiesen, wenn es müde war.

Das war alles vor dem Krieg.

Franz Marc, der blaue Reiter vom Ried,
Stieg auf sein Kriegspferd.
Ritt über Benediktbeuern herab nach Unterbayern,
Neben ihm sein besonnener, treuer Nubier
Hält ihm die Waffe.

FRANZ MARC

The Blue Rider has fallen in battle, a great Biblical figure, about whom the fragrance of Eden hung. Over the landscape his blue shadow fell. He was the one who could still hear the animals speak; and he transfigured their uncomprehended souls. The Blue Rider from the war always reminded me of that: it does not suffice alone to be kind to human beings, and the good that you do to the horses, since they must suffer unspeakably on the battlefield, you also do to me.

He is dead. Great angels bore his giant body to God, who holds his blue soul in His hand, like a glowing flag. I think of a story in the Talmud that a priest once told to me: how God stood in front of the ruined temple with men and wept. For wherever the Blue Rider went he made a gift of heaven. So many birds fly through the night; they can still play wind and breath, but we know nothing more about that down here; we can only chop each other to bits or indifferently pass each other by. In this soberness an immense blood-mill is raised up threateningly, and we people all will soon be crushed. Stride perpetually across the waiting earth. The Blue Rider has arrived; he was still too young to die.

I never saw any painter paint softer and with greater godlike seriousness than he. "Lemon oxen" and "burning buffaloes" was what he called his animals, and a star ascended on his brow. But the animals of the wilderness, they too, began to become like plants in his tropical hand. He enchanted tigresses into anemones; around panthers he hung the jewels of the gillyflower; he spoke of *pure* slaughter when, in his pictures, a panther brought down a gazelle from the cliffs. He felt himself like a young arch-father in Biblical times, a splendid Jacob he, the Prince of Cana. Wildly he folded the thicket around his shoulders; his beautiful face he mirrored in the spring, and often he bore his miraculous heart wrapped up in fur, home like a sleeping boy-child, over the meadows when it was tired.

That was all before the war.

Franz Marc, the Blue Rider of Ried,
Mounted his war horse.
Rode over Benediktbeuern down into Lower Bavaria;
Beside him his prudent, loyal Nubian
Carries his weapon.

Aber um seinen Hals trägt er mein silbergeprägtes Bild
Und den todverhütenden Stein seines teuren Weibes.
Durch die Straßen von München hebt er sein biblisches Haupt
Im hellen Rahmen des Himmels.
Trost im stillenden Mandelauge,
Donner sein Herz.
Hinter ihm und zur Seite viele, viele Soldaten.

MEIN KIND

Mein Kind schreit auf um die Mitternacht
Und ist so heiß aus dem Traum erwacht.

Gäb ihm so gern meines Blutes Mai,
Spräng nur mein bebendes Herz entzwei.

Der Tod schleicht im Hyänenfell
Am Himmelsstreif im Mondeshell.

Aber die Erde im Blütenkeusch
Singt Lenz im kreisenden Weltgeräusch.

Und wundersüß küßt der Maienwind
Als duftender Gottesbote mein Kind.

But around his neck he wears my picture in silver
And the death-averting stone of his precious wife.
Through the streets of Munich he lifts his Biblical head
In the brilliant frame of the sky.
Solace in his silencing almond eye,
Thunder his heart.
Behind him and at his side many, many soldiers.

MY CHILD

I hear my child at midnight scream,
Awakened from the sweat of dream.

The May of my blood he could gladly take
If only my throbbing heart would break.

Death slinks in a hyena's skin
Through the bright moonlight on the heaven's rim.

But the earth, in budding chasteness furled,
Sings Spring in the sound of the circling world.

And wonderfully sweet the May wind nods
To kiss my child like a breath from the gods.

DIE PAVIANMUTTER
SINGT IHR PAVIÄNCHEN IN DEN SCHLAF
(Wiegenliedchen)

Schlafe, schlafe,
Mein Rosenpöpöchen,
Mein Zuckerläuschen,
Mein Goldflöhchen,

Morgen wird die Kaiserin aus Asien kommen
Mit Zucker, Schokoladen und Bombommen,

Schnell, schnell,
Haase Haase machen,
Sonst kriegt Blaumäulchen nichts von den Sachen.

ANTINOUS

Der kleine Süßkönig
Muß mit goldenen Bällen spielen.

Im bunten Brunnen
Blaugeträufel, honiggold,
Seine Spielehände kühlen.

Antinous,
Wildfang, Güldklang,
Kuchenkorn mahlen alle Mühlen.

Antinous,
Du kleiner Spielkönig,
In den Himmel fährt es schön auf Schaukelstühlen.

O, wie lustige Falter seine Augen sind
Und die Schelme all in seiner Wange,
Und sein Herzchen beißt, will mans befühlen.

THE BABOON MOTHER
SINGS HER BABOONLET TO SLEEP
(Lullaby)

Sleep, go to sleep,
My little rose bottom,
My little sugar louse,
My dear little flea,

The Empress of Asia will come tomorrow
With sugar, candy, and chocolorrow,

Quick, quick,
Make Bunny Bunny
Or little blue-mouth gets none of the honey.

ANTINOUS

The little sweet-king
Must play with golden balls.

In the bright fountain
Blue-trickle, honey-gold,
His play-hands are cooling.

Antinous,
Mad-cap, gilt-sound,
All the mills grind cake-grain.

Antinous,
You little play-king,
It's a fine ride to heaven in rocking chairs.

Oh, what funny butterflies his eyes are
And all the rogues in his cheek,
And his heart bites, if you try to feel it.

MEIN STILLES LIED

Mein Herz ist eine traurige Zeit,
Die tonlos tickt.

Meine Mutter hatte goldene Flügel,
Die keine Welt fanden.

Horcht, mich sucht meine Mutter,
Lichte sind ihre Finger und ihre Füße wandernde Träume.

Und süße Wetter mit blauen Wehen
Wärmen meine Schlummer

Immer in den Nächten,
Deren Tage meiner Mutter Krone tragen.

Und ich trinke aus dem Monde stillen Wein,
Wenn die Nacht einsam kommt.

Meine Lieder trugen des Sommers Bläue
Und kehrten düster heim.

—Ihr verhöhntet meine Lippe
Und redet mit ihr.—

Doch ich griff nach euren Händen,
Denn meine Liebe ist ein Kind und wollte spielen.

Und ich artete mich nach euch,
Weil ich mich nach dem Menschen sehnte.

Arm bin ich geworden
An eurer bettelnden Wohltat.

Und das Meer wird es wehklagen
Gott.

Ich bin der Hieroglyph,
Der unter der Schöpfung steht

Und mein Auge
Ist der Gipfel der Zeit;

Sein Leuchten küßt Gottes Saum.

MY QUIET SONG
(Second Version)

My heart is a sad time
Tonelessly ticking.

My mother had golden wings
That found no world.

Listen! My mother's looking for me;
Her fingers are candles, her feet are wandering dreams.

And sweet weathers with blue winds
Warm my slumber

In the nights always
Whose days are wearing my mother's crown.

And from the moon I drink a quiet wine
When the night comes lonely.

My songs carried the summer's blue
And gloomily turned home.

—You scorned my lip
And speak with it.—

But I reached for your hands,
For my love is a child and wanted to play.

And I assumed your ways
Because I longed for human kind.

I have become poor
From your begging benefaction.

And the ocean will lament it
Unto God.

I am the hieroglyph
Inscribed beneath creation.

And my eye
Is the pinnacle of time;

Its lusters kiss God's hem.

GEBET

Ich suche allerlanden eine Stadt,
Die einen Engel vor der Pforte hat.
Ich trage seinen großen Flügel
Gebrochen schwer am Schulterblatt
Und in der Stirne seinen Stern als Siegel.

Und wandle immer in die Nacht . . .
Ich habe Liebe in die Welt gebracht—
Daß blau zu blühen jedes Herz vermag,
Und hab ein Leben müde mich gewacht,
In Gott gehüllt den dunklen Atemschlag.

O Gott, schließ um mich deinen Mantel fest;
Ich weiß, ich bin im Kugelglas der Rest,
Und wenn der letzte Mensch die Welt vergießt,
Du mich nicht wieder aus der Allmacht läßt
Und sich ein neuer Erdball um mich schließt.

PRAYER

I'm searching for a city in these lands
Before whose gate a mighty angel stands;
For, broken at the shoulder blade,
I bear his wings' gigantic spans,
And on my brow his star as seal is laid.

And always wander in the night . . .
I brought love to the world, and light—
So every heart can blossom forth in blue;
And with my darkened breath cloaked in God's might,
I have kept weary watch my whole life through.

O God, wrap up your robe around me fast:
I know I'm just the drop left in the glass.
And as the last man stands pouring out the world,
Out of your power you'll never let me pass,
And a new globe around me will be furled.

VERSÖHNUNG

Es wird ein großer Stern in meinen Schoß fallen . . .
Wir wollen wachen die Nacht,

In den Sprachen beten,
Die wie Harfen eingeschnitten sind.

Wir wollen uns versöhnen die Nacht—
So viel Gott strömt über.

Kinder sind unsere Herzen,
Die möchten ruhen müdesüß.

Und unsere Lippen wollen sich küssen,
Was zagst du?

Grenzt nicht mein Herz an deins—
Immer färbt dein Blut meine Wangen rot.

Wir wollen uns versöhnen die Nacht,
Wenn wir uns herzen, sterben wir nicht.

Es wird ein großer Stern in meinen Schoß fallen.

RECONCILIATION

There will be a giant star fall in my womb . . .
Let us wake through the night,

Pray in the languages
That are incised like harps.

Let us be reconciled in the night—
So much God flows over.

Our hearts are child and child,
They'd like to rest so weary-sweet.

And our lips want to kiss one another,
Why do you wait?

Doesn't my heart border yours—
Your blood always colors my cheeks red.

Let us be reconciled in the night,
Whenever we embrace we do not die.

There will be a giant star fall in my womb.

MEIN VOLK

Der Fels wird morsch,
Dem ich entspringe
Und meine Gotteslieder singe ...
Jäh stürz ich vom Weg
Und riesele ganz in mir
Fernab, allein über Klagegestein
Dem Meer zu.

Hab mich so abgeströmt
Von meines Blutes
Mostvergorenheit.
Und immer, immer noch der Widerhall
In mir,
Wenn schauerlich gen Ost
Das morsche Felsgebein,
Mein Volk,
Zu Gott schreit.

MY PEOPLE

The rock begins to crack
From which I spring
And my divine songs sing . . .
Steep from the path I plunge
And trickle, all in me,
Far off, alone over grieving stone,
Toward the sea.

So much I've streamed away
Of my blood's
Early fermentation.
And always and again the echoing
In me,
When shuddering towards the East
The crumbling skeleton of stone,
My people
Cries to God.

ABEL

Kains Augen sind nicht gottwohlgefällig,
Abels Angesicht ist ein goldener Garten,
Abels Augen sind Nachtigallen.

Immer singt Abel so hell
Zu den Saiten seiner Seele,
Aber durch Kains Leib führen die Gräben der Stadt.

Und er wird seinen Bruder erschlagen—
Abel, Abel, dein Blut färbt den Himmel tief.

Wo ist Kain, da ich ihn stürmen will:
Hast du die Süßvögel erschlagen
In deines Bruders Angesicht?!!

ABEL

Cain's eyes are not well pleasing unto God;
But a golden garden is Abel's countenance;
Abel's eyes are nightingales.

So brightly does Abel always sing
To the strings of his soul
But the city ditches pass through the body of Cain.

And he'll slay his brother—
Abel, Abel, your blood will deeply dye the sky.

Where is Cain, for I would storm him:
Did you slay the sweet-bird
In the face of your brother?!!

ABRAHAM UND ISAAK

Abraham baute in der Landschaft Eden
Sich eine Stadt aus Erde und aus Blatt
Und übte sich mit Gott zu reden.

Die Engel ruhten gern vor seiner frommen Hütte
Und Abraham erkannte jeden;
Himmlische Zeichen ließen ihre Flügelschritte.

Bis sie dann einmal bang in ihren Träumen
Meckern hörten die gequälten Böcke,
Mit denen Isaak Opfern spielte hinter Süßholzbäumen.

Und Gott ermahnte: Abraham!!
Er brach vom Kamm des Meeres Muscheln ab und Schwamm
Hoch auf den Blöcken den Altar zu schmücken.

Und trug den einzigen Sohn gebunden auf den Rücken
Zu werden seinem großen Herrn gerecht—
Der aber liebte seinen Knecht.

ABRAHAM AND ISAAC

Abraham built himself on Eden's sod
A city raised of earth and leaf
And practiced converse with his God.

The angels pleased to rest before his holy home
And Abraham knew every one;
Their wingèd steps left symbols in the loam.

Until they then once heard in fearful dreams
The bleating of tormented rams
Where Isaac was playing sacrifice behind the licorice trees.

And God admonished: Abraham!
From the ridge of the sea he broke off sponge and clam
To trim the altar towering up in stone.

And bound on his back he bore his only son
Since that his Lord's command did him compel—
The Lord, however, loved his servant well.

HAGAR UND ISMAEL

Mit Muscheln spielten Abrahams kleine Söhne
Und ließen schwimmen die Perlmutterkähne;
Dann lehnte Isaak bang sich an den Ismael

Und traurig sangen die zwei schwarzen Schwäne
Um ihre bunte Welt ganz dunkle Töne,
Und die verstoßne Hagar raubte ihren Sohn sich schnell.

Vergoß in seine kleine ihre große Träne,
Und ihre Herzen rauschten wie der heilige Quell,
Und übereilten noch die Straußenhähne.

Die Sonne aber brannte auf die Wüste grell
Und Hagar und ihr Knäblein sanken in das gelbe Fell
Und bissen in den heißen Sand die weißen Negerzähne.

JAKOB UND ESAU

Rebekkas Magd ist eine himmlische Fremde,
Aus Rosenblättern trägt die Engelin ein Hemde
Und einen Stern im Angesicht.

Und immer blickt sie auf zum Licht,
Und ihre sanften Hände lesen
Aus goldenen Linsen ein Gericht.

Jakob und Esau blühn an ihrem Wesen
Und streiten um die Süßigkeiten nicht,
Die sie in ihrem Schoß zum Mahle bricht.

Der Bruder läßt dem jüngeren die Jagd
Und all sein Erbe für den Dienst der Magd;
Um seine Schultern schlägt er wild das Dickicht.

HAGAR AND ISHMAEL

The little sons of Abraham took shells
And floated boats made out of mother-pearl;
Then Isaac leaned in fear on Ishmael.

And mournfully sang the two black swans
Quite gloomy notes around their brilliant world,
And the banished Hagar quickly stole her son.

Poured into his small tear her larger one,
And their hearts murmured like a sacred well
And could the swiftest ostriches outrun.

But the sun on the desert dazzled like a brand,
And into its yellow fur the boy and Hagar fell
And their white negroes' teeth bit burning sand.

JACOB AND ESAU

Rebecca's maiden is a heavenly stranger.
A garment of rose petals garbs the angel
And in her face a star.

And she looks upward at the light afar,
And her soft hands and gentle
Are shelling a pottage of golden lentil.

Jacob and Esau blossom from her being,
Nor seek those sweetnesses with quarrelsome zeal,
That in her lap she breaks to make the meal.

One brother sells the younger undismayed,
His hunt and heritage to serve the maid;
Bursts shouldering through the thicket and away.

JAKOB

Jakob war der Büffel seiner Herde.
Wenn er stampfte mit den Hufen,
Sprühte unter ihm die Erde.

Brüllend ließ er die gescheckten Brüder.
Rannte in den Urwald an die Flüsse,
Stillte dort das Blut der Affenbisse.

Durch die müden Schmerzen in den Knöcheln
Sank er vor dem Himmel fiebernd nieder,
Und sein Ochsgesicht erschuf das Lächeln.

JACOB

Jacob was the buffalo of his herd.
When he thundered with his hooves
Earth beneath him rocked and stirred.

Bellowed, left his many-colored brothers,
Ran through jungle to the cool lagoons,
Staunched the blood there of his ape-bite wounds.

Fever forced him to sink down a while
Under heaven, to rest his painful bones;
And his ox-face bore the world's first smile.

PHARAO UND JOSEPH

Pharao verstößt seine blühenden Weiber,
Sie duften nach den Gärten Amons.

Sein Königskopf ruht auf meiner Schulter,
Die strömt Korngeruch aus.

Pharao ist von Gold.
Seine Augen gehen und kommen
Wie schillernde Nilwellen.

Sein Herz aber liegt in meinem Blut;
Zehn Wölfe gingen an meine Tränke.

Immer denkt Pharao
An meine Brüder,
Die mich in die Grube warfen.

Säulen werden im Schlaf seine Arme
Und drohen!

Aber sein träumerisch Herz
Rauscht auf meinem Grund.

Darum dichten meine Lippen
Große Süßigkeiten,
Im Weizen unseres Morgens.

PHARAOH AND JOSEPH

Pharaoh dismisses his blossoming wives;
They are fragrant as Amon's gardens.

His royal head rests upon my shoulder,
Which sends forth the scent of grain.

Pharaoh is golden.
His eyes come and go
Like shimmering waves of the Nile.

His heart, though, lies in my blood;
Ten wolves went to my watering place.

Pharaoh thinks always
Upon my brothers
Who cast me into the pit.

In sleep his arms become pillars
And threaten!

But his dreamer's heart
Roars on my riverbed.

Wherefore my lips are thick with words
Of very sweetness
In the wheat of our morn.

MOSES UND JOSUA

Als Moses im Alter Gottes war,
Nahm er den wilden Juden Josua
Und salbte ihn zum König seiner Schar.

Da ging ein Sehnen weich durch Israel—
Denn Josuas Herz erquickte wie ein Quell.
Des Bibelvolkes Judenleib war sein Altar.

Die Mägde mochten den gekrönten Bruder gern—
Wie heiliger Dornstrauch brannte süß sein Haar;
Sein Lächeln grüßte den ersehnten Heimatstern,

Den Mosis altes Sterbeauge aufgehn sah,
Als seine müde Löwenseele schrie zum Herrn.

MOSES AND JOSHUA

When Moses was as old as God
He took the wild Jew Joshua
And anointed him king of his multitudes.

Then a soft longing went through Israel,
For Joshua's heart refreshed them like a well.
His altar was the body of the Bible's Jews.

With maidens the brother king was popular—
Like holy thornbush did his hair burn sweet;
His smile did greet the homeland's beckoning star,

Which Moses' dying eye still lived to see
When his tired lion's soul cried out to God.

DAVID UND JONATHAN

In der Bibel stehn wir geschrieben
Buntumschlungen.

Aber unsere Knabenspiele
Leben weiter im Stern.

Ich bin David,
Du mein Spielgefährte.

O, wir färbten
Unsere weißen Widderherzen rot!

Wie die Knospen an den Liebespsalmen
Unter Feiertagshimmel.

Deine Abschiedsaugen aber—
Immer nimmst du still im Kusse Abschied.

Und was soll dein Herz
Noch ohne meines—

Deine Süßnacht
Ohne meine Lieder.

DAVID AND JONATHAN

In the Bible we are written
In bright embrace.

But our boyish games
Survive in the star.

I am David.
You my playmate.

Oh, we dyed
Our white ram-hearts red!

Like the buds on the love-psalms
Beneath holiday skies.

But your leave-taking eyes—
You always depart with a wordless kiss.

And what should your heart do
Without mine too—

Your sweet night
Without my song.

DAVID UND JONATHAN

O Jonathan, ich blasse hin in deinem Schoß,
Mein Herz fällt feierlich in dunklen Falten;
In meiner Schläfe pflege du den Mond,
Des Sternes Gold sollst du erhalten.
Du bist mein Himmel mein, du Liebgenoß.

Ich hab so säumerisch die kühle Welt
Fern immer nur im Bach geschaut . . .
Doch nun, da sie aus meinem Auge fällt,
Von deiner Liebe aufgetaut . . .
O Jonathan, nimm du die königliche Träne,
Sie schimmert weich und reich wie eine Braut.

O Jonathan, du Blut der süßen Feige,
Duftendes Gehang an meinem Zweige,
Du Ring in meiner Lippe Haut.

ESTHER

Esther ist schlank wie die Feldpalme,
Nach ihren Lippen duften die Weizenhalme
Und die Feiertage, die in Juda fallen.

Nachts ruht ihr Herz auf einem Psalme,
Die Götzen lauschen in den Hallen.

Der König lächelt ihrem Nahen entgegen—
Denn überall blickt Gott auf Esther.

Die jungen Juden dichten Lieder an die Schwester,
Die sie in Säulen ihres Vorraums prägen.

DAVID AND JONATHAN

O Jonathan, I pale in your embrace;
My heart is draped in dark and solemn folds.
In the temple of my brow—care for the moon!
And from the stars receive their gold!
You are my heaven, mine, you mate of grace.

I've only viewed the cool world in the streams,
Indolent, as if from far above . . .
But since in my eye it now no longer gleams,
Being thawed out by your love . . .
O Jonathan, you, take the royal tear!
It shines rich as a bride, soft as a dove.

O Jonathan, you blood of the sweet fig,
You aromatic pendant on my twig,
You ring, through my lip interwove.

ESTHER

Esther is slender as a palm.
The blades of wheat take from her lips their balm,
And the feast days that in Judah fall.

At night her heart reposes on a psalm;
The idols hearken in the hall.

The king looks, smiling, when she comes—
For everywhere God watches Esther.

The young Jews compose love songs to their sister,
Which they incise in the pillars before her room.

ZEBAOTH

Gott, ich liebe dich in deinem Rosenkleide,
Wenn du aus den Gärten trittst, Zebaoth.
O, du Gottjüngling,
Du Dichter,
Ich trinke einsam von deinen Düften.

Meine erste Blüte Blut sehnte sich nach dir,
So komme doch,
Du süßer Gott,
Du Gespiele Gott,
Deines Tores Gold schmilzt an meiner Sehnsucht.

ABSCHIED

Der Regen säuberte die steile Häuserwand,
Ich schreibe auf den weißen, steinernen Bogen
Und fühle sanft erstarken meine müde Hand
Von Liebesversen, die mich immer süß betrogen.

Ich wache in der Nacht stürmisch auf hohen Meereswogen!
Vielleicht entglitt ich meines Engels liebevoller Hand,
Ich hab' die Welt, die Welt hat mich betrogen;
Ich grub den Leichnam zu den Muscheln in den Sand.

Wir blicken all' zu *einem* Himmel auf, mißgönnen uns das Land?—
Warum hat Gott im Osten wetterleuchtend sich verzogen,
Vom Ebenbilde Seines Menschen übermannt?

Ich wache in der Nacht stürmisch auf hohen Meereswogen!
Und was mich je mit Seiner Schöpfung Ruhetag verband,
Ist wie ein spätes Adlerheer unstät in diese Dunkelheit geflogen.

SABAOTH

God but I love you in your robe of rose
When you come from the garden, Sabaoth.
O godlike youth,
You poet;
Lonely, I drink of your fragrances.

My first bud of blood was a yearning for you;
So come then,
You sweet god,
You playmate god,
The gold of your gate will melt from my longing.

DEPARTURE

The rain cleaned off the steep facade of houses;
I write upon the white and stony sheet
And feel how my tired hand so softly rouses
From love poems that always, sweetly, were a cheat.

I wake in the stormy night, on high waves of the sea!
Perhaps I have slipped from my angel's loving hand;
I cheated the world, and the world has cheated me;
I buried the corpse with the seashells in the sand.

We all look up to a *single* heaven, begrudge each other land?
Why has God drawn away with lightning toward the East,
By the image of His human being outmanned?

I wake in the stormy night, on high waves of the sea!
What bound me to the Day of Rest when His creation ceased
Has flown, like a late eagle-army, into this dark unsteadily.

DAS WUNDERLIED

Schwärmend trat ich aus glitzerndem Herzen
Wogender Liebesfäden,

Ganz schüchtern, hervor; Nacht im Auge,
Geöffnete Lippen . . .

Aber wo auch ein See lockte,
Goldene Tränke,

Starb an der Labe mein pochendes Wild
In der Brust.

Was soll mir der Wein deines Tisches,
Reichst du mir des Herzens Mannah nicht.

Süß mir, wenn ich im Rauschen der Liebe
Für dich gestorben wär—

Nun ist mein Leben verschneit,
Erstarrt meine Seele,

Die lächelte sonntäglich dir
Friede ins Herz.

Ich suche das Glück nicht mehr.
Wo ich auch unter hochzeitlichem Morgen saß,

Erfror der träumende Lotos
Auf meinem Blut.

THE SONG OF WONDER

In rapture and from the glittering heart
Of billowing love-strings

Shyly I stepped forth; night in my eye,
Lips open . . .

But wherever a lake lured,
Golden waters,

There died of refreshment the throbbing deer
In my wild breast.

What use is the wine of your table to me
If you don't serve the manna of your heart.

Sweet for me, if in the rush of love,
I had died for you.

Snow falls on my life now,
Numb my soul;

It sent a Sunday smile of peace
Into your heart.

Happiness I no longer seek.
Wherever under the wedding morn I sat,

The dreaming lotus froze
Upon my blood.

GOTT HÖR ...

Um meine Augen zieht die Nacht sich
Wie ein Ring zusammen.
Mein Puls verwandelte das Blut in Flammen
Und doch war alles grau und kalt um mich.

O Gott und bei lebendigem Tage,
Träum ich vom Tod.
Im Wasser trink ich ihn und würge ihn im Brot.
Für meine Traurigkeit gibt es kein Maß auf deiner Waage.

Gott hör ... In deiner blauen Lieblingsfarbe
Sang ich das Lied von deines Himmels Dach—
Und weckte doch in deinem ewigen Hauche nicht den Tag.
Mein Herz schämt sich vor dir fast seiner tauben Narbe.

Wo ende ich? —O Gott!! Denn in die Sterne,
Auch in den Mond sah ich, in alle deiner Früchte Tal.
Der rote Wein wird schon in seiner Beere schal ...
Und überall—die Bitternis—in jedem Kerne.

GOD, HEAR...

The night draws in around my eyes
Its ring of haze.
My pulse has sent my blood into a blaze
Though all about me a gray coldness lies.

O God, that I by living day
Should dream I'm dead,
Drink it in water, choke on it in my bread.
There's no measure of my grief your scale can weigh.

God, hear . . . in your own favorite color blue
I sang the song of the roof of your sky—
Yet, in your endless breath, I could not wake the day.
With its dull scar my heart's almost ashamed to come to you.

Where will I end? —O God!! For into the stars,
Also into the moon I looked, into your fruitful vale.
Even in the very berry the red wine grows stale . . .
And everywhere—the bitterness—at the core.

ABENDLIED

Auf die jungen Rosensträucher
Fällt vom Himmel weicher Regen,
Und die Welt wird immer reicher.

O mein Gott mein, nur alleine,
Ich verdurste und verweine
In dem Segen.

Engel singen aus den Höhen:
»Heut ist Gottes Namenstag,
Der allweiß hier vom Geschehen . . .«

Und ich kann es nicht verstehen,
Da ich unter seinem Dach
Oft so traurig erwach.

WEIHNACHTEN

Einmal kommst du zu mir in der Abendstunde
Aus meinem Lieblingssterne weich entrückt
Das ersehnte Liebeswort im Munde
Alle Zweige warten schon geschmückt.

O ich weiß, ich leuchte wieder dann,
Denn du zündest meine weißen Lichte an.

»Wann?« —ich frage seit ich dir begegnet— »wann?»
Einen Engel schnitt ich mir aus deinem goldenen Haare
Und den Traum, der mir so früh zerrann.
O ich liebe dich, ich liebe dich,
Ich liebe dich!

Hörst du, ich liebe dich———
Und unsere Liebe wandelt schon Kometenjahre,
Bevor du mich erkanntest und ich dich.

EVENING SONG

Soft the rain and never ceases,
Falls from heaven on young roses,
And the world's wealth still increases.

O my God, mine, I alone
Die of thirst and always moan
In its riches.

From on high the angels sing:
"Today's God's birthday celebration,
Who all-knows what's happening . . ."

And I cannot understand it,
Since so often in His room
I awaken full of gloom.

CHRISTMAS

Someday you'll come to me at the hour of eve,
Softly rapt away from my favorite star,
Speaking the word of love I crave to receive;
My branches in their finery watch the door.

Oh, I know that I'll be glowing then,
Since you'll light my candles once again.

"When?" —I've been asking since I met you —"when?"
I clipped myself an angel from your golden hair
And the dream that fled so soon again.
Oh, I love you, I love you,
I love you!

Are you listening, I love you———
And our love had been wandering on for comets' years
Before you recognized me and I you.

GENESIS

Aus Algenmoos und Muscheln schleichen feuchte Düfte . . .
Frohlockend schmiegt die Erde ihren Arm um meine Hüfte.
—Mein Geist hat nach dem Heiligen Geist gesucht—.

Und tauchte auf den Vogelgrund der Lüfte
Und grub nach Gott in jedem Stein der Klüfte
Und blieb doch Fleisch, leibeigen und verflucht.

Ich keimte schon am Zweig der Liebesgifte,
Als noch der Schöpfer durch die Meere schiffte,
Das Wasser trennte von der Bucht.

Und alles gut fand, da Er Seine Erde prüfte,
Und nicht ein Korn sprießt ungebucht.

Doch Seine beiden Menschen trieb Er in die Flucht!
Noch schlief der Weltenplan in Seinem Schöpferstifte.
Sie fügten sich nicht Seiner väterlichen Zucht.

Unbändig wie das Feuer zwischen Stein und Stein
Noch ungeläutert zu entladen sich versucht,
So trotzten sie!!
Wie meines Herzens ungezähmte Wucht.

GENESIS

Damp exhalations creep from shell and weedy sea . . .
Around my hip clings the earth's arm, exultantly.
—My spirit sought the Holy Spirit's light.

And dipped into the bird-vale of the air,
And dug for God in stone cliffs everywhere
And yet remained but flesh, in thralldom to the night.

I budded on the branch of love's dread potion,
While still the Creator sailed across the ocean,
Dividing the water from the bight,

And, when He judged His earth, found good the notion.
And not a seed springs up beyond His sight.

Yet did He put His human pair to flight!
His pen that planned the world had not yet waked to motion.
For they would not submit to His paternal right.

Unruly as the fire between a stone and stone
Attempts unpurified to come alight,
They bid defiance!
Like the force of my own heart's unbridled spite.

JERUSALEM
Gott baute aus Seinem Rückgrat: Palästina
aus einem einzigen Knochen: Jerusalem.

Ich wandele wie durch Mausoleen—
Versteint ist unsere Heilige Stadt.
Es ruhen Steine in den Betten ihrer toten Seen
Statt Wasserseiden, die da spielten: Kommen und Vergehen.

Es starren Gründe hart den Wanderer an—
Und er versinkt in ihre starren Nächte.
Ich habe Angst, die ich nicht überwältigen kann.

Wenn du doch kämest. . . .
Im lichten Alpenmantel eingehüllt—
Und meines Tages Dämmerstunde nähmest—
Mein Arm umrahmte dich, ein hilfreich Heiligenbild.

Wie einst wenn ich im Dunkel meines Herzens litt—
Da deine Augen beide: blaue Wolken.
Sie nahmen mich aus meinem Trübsinn mit.

Wenn du doch kämest—
In das Land der Ahnen—
Du würdest wie ein Kindlein mich ermahnen:
Jerusalem—erfahre Auferstehen!

Es grüßen uns
Des »Einzigen Gottes« lebendige Fahnen,
Grünende Hände, die des Lebens Odem säen.

JERUSALEM
God built out of His spine: Palestine
out of a single bone: Jerusalem

They are like mausoleums where I stray—
Our Holy City has turned to stone.
Stones rest in the beds where once its dead lakes lay
Instead of the water-silks that played there: come and pass away.

Beneath the wanderer the hard valleys lower—
And he sinks downward in their rigid nights.
I feel a fear I cannot overpower.

If you but came. . . .
With your bright Alpine mantle wrapped around you—
And took the twilight hour of my day—
For your helpful, saintly icon my arm would be a frame.

Like once when I was suffering in the darkness of my heart—
Since both your eyes: blue clouds.
They took me away from my gloominess.

If you but came—
To the forefathers' land—
You would admonish me just like a child:
Jerusalem—experience resurrection!

We're greeted by
The living flags of the "Only God,"
Greening hands that sow the breath of life.

AN MEIN KIND

Immer wieder wirst du mir
Im scheidenden Jahre sterben, mein Kind,

Wenn das Laub zerfließt
Und die Zweige schmal werden.

Mit den roten Rosen
Hast du den Tod bitter gekostet,

Nicht ein einziges welkendes Pochen
Blieb dir erspart.

Darum weine ich sehr, ewiglich. . . .
In der Nacht meines Herzens.

Noch seufzen aus mir die Schlummerlieder,
Die dich in den Todesschlaf schluchzten,

Und meine Augen wenden sich nicht mehr
Der Welt zu;

Das Grün des Laubes tut ihnen weh.
—Aber der Ewige wohnt in mir.

Die Liebe zu dir ist das Bildnis,
Das man sich von Gott machen darf.

Ich sah auch die Engel im Weinen,
Im Wind und im Schneeregen.

Sie schwebten . . . .
In einer himmlischen Luft.

Wenn der Mond in Blüte steht
Gleicht er deinem Leben, mein Kind.

Und ich mag nicht hinsehen
Wie der lichtspendende Falter sorglos dahinschwebt.

Nie ahnte ich den Tod
—Spüren um dich, mein Kind—

TO MY CHILD

Over and over again you'll die
Away from me in the parting year, my child.

When the leaves flow down
And the branches all turn slender.

Like the rose once red
Death you have tasted bitterly,

You were not spared a single
Wilting throb.

That's why I cry aloud, eternally. . . .
In the nighttime of my heart.

The lullabies still come sighing out from me
Which sobbed you to death's sleep,

And my eyes no longer turn
Towards the world;

The green of the leaves is hurtful to them.
—But the Eternal One resides in me.

My love of you is the image
That one is allowed to make of God.

I saw the angels weeping too,
In the wind and the snowy rain.

They hovered there . . .
In a heavenly breeze.

When the moon stands blooming
It's like your life, my child.

And I don't want to watch
How the light-shedding butterfly floats carefree on.

I never suspected death
—Scenting you out, my child—

Und ich liebe des Zimmers Wände,
Die ich bemale mit deinem Knabenantlitz.

Die Sterne, die in diesem Monat
So viele sprühend ins Leben fallen,
Tropfen schwer auf mein Herz.

MEIN BLAUES KLAVIER

Ich habe zu Hause ein blaues Klavier
Und kenne doch keine Note.

Es steht im Dunkel der Kellertür,
Seitdem die Welt verrohte.

Es spielen Sternenhände vier
—Die Mondfrau sang im Boote—
Nun tanzen die Ratten im Geklirr.

Zerbrochen ist die Klaviatür. . . .
Ich beweine die blaue Tote.

Ach liebe Engel öffnet mir
—Ich aß vom bitteren Brote—
Mir lebend schon die Himmelstür—
Auch wider dem Verbote.

And I love the walls of the room,
Which I am painting with your boyish face.

The stars that in this month
So many sparkling fall in life
Drop heavy on my heart.

MY BLUE PIANO

I have at my house still a blue piano
And yet cannot play a note.

In the dark of the cellar door it stands
Since the world filled with brutal folk.

Star-hands four are playing there
—The moon-woman sang in the boat—
Now the rats are dancing in its blare.

The keyboard is broken beyond repair. . . .
I weep for the blue departed.

Ah, open to me, angels fair,
—I ate of the bitter bread—
To me, still living, heaven's door—
Though it be prohibited.

GEBET

Oh Gott, ich bin voll Traurigkeit. . . .
Nimm mein Herz in deine Hände—
Bis der Abend geht zu Ende
In steter Wiederkehr der Zeit.

Oh Gott, ich bin so müd, oh, Gott,
Der Wolkenmann und seine Frau
Sie spielen mit mir himmelblau
Im Sommer immer, lieber Gott.

Und glaube unserm Monde, Gott,
Denn er umhüllte mich mit Schein,
Als wär ich hilflos noch und klein,
—Ein Flämmchen Seele.

Oh, Gott und ist sie auch voll Fehle—
Nimm sie still in deine Hände. . . .
Damit sie leuchtend in dir ende.

PRAYER

O God, I'm full of dull concern. . . .
Take my heart into your hands—
Until the evening finally ends
In time's continual return.

O God, I am so tired, oh, God,
The cloudman and his goodwife too
They're playing with me heavenly blue
Always in summer, dearest God.

And please believe our moon, O God,
For he has bundled me in light
As if I were small and helpless quite,
—A little flame of soul.

O God, though it of fault be full—
Take it quietly in your hand. . . .
That, in you, it may gleam—and end.

OUVERTÜRE

Wir trennten uns im Vorspiele der Liebe. . . .
An meinem Herzen glitzerte noch hell dein Wort,
Und still verklangen wir im Stadtgetriebe,
Im Abendschleier der Septembertrübe
In einem schluchzenden Akkord.
Doch in der kurzen Liebesouvertüre
Entschwanden wir von dieser Erde fort
Durch Paradiese bis zur Himmelstüre—
Und es bedurfte nicht der ewigen Liebesschwüre
Und nicht der Küsse blauer Zaubermord.
Und meiden doch seitdem uns wie zwei Diebe!
Und nur geheim betreten wir den Ort,
Wo uns vergoldete die Liebe.
Bewahren wir sie, daß sie nicht erfriere
Oder im Alltag blinder Lust verdorrt.
Ich weinte bitterlich wenn ich es einst erführe—

OVERTURE

We parted early in the game of love. . . .
Your word still glittered brightly on my heart,
And, silent, we faded in the city's horde,
In dull September's evening veil
With a sobbing, musical accord.
And yet in that brief overture of love
We vanished from this earth entire away
Through paradises up to heaven's door—
And felt no need, nor love-eternal swore,
Nor did blue magic murder in a kiss.
And still we avoid each other since like thieves!
And the place love gilded us with bliss
We enter only by a secret way.
Let us preserve our love, that it not freeze
Or fade, in the blind pleasure of everyday.
I'd weep bitter tears if it ever turned out that way.

DIE VERSCHEUCHTE

Es ist der Tag im Nebel völlig eingehüllt,
Entseelt begegnen alle Welten sich—
Kaum hingezeichnet wie auf einem Schattenbild.

Wie lange war kein Herz zu meinem mild . . .
Die Welt erkaltete, der Mensch verblich.
—Komm bete mit mir—denn Gott tröstet mich.

Wo weilt der Odem, der aus meinem Leben wich?
Ich streife heimatlos zusammen mit dem Wild
Durch bleiche Zeiten träumend—ja ich liebte dich. . . .

Wo soll ich hin, wenn kalt der Nordsturm brüllt?
Die scheuen Tiere aus der Landschaft wagen sich
Und ich vor deine Tür, ein Bündel Wegerich.

Bald haben Tränen alle Himmel weggespült,
An deren Kelchen Dichter ihren Durst gestillt—
Auch du und ich.

CHASED AWAY

The day's quite shrouded in with fog and wet.
The worlds all meet each other lifelessly—
Barely outlined, as in a silhouette.

How long no heart has treated mine with care . . .
The world became quite cold, and mankind paled.
—Come pray with me—God comforts my despair.

The spirit that fled my life, where does it dwell?
Homeless I rove together with the deer
Through pale times dreaming—yes, I loved you well. . . .

Where shall I go, when the cold north wind roars?
Out of the landscape shy things venture forth
And I before your door, a clump of wayside flowers.

My tears will soon have washed away the sky
Whose chalices once stilled the poets' thirst—
And you and I.

HINGABE

Ich sehe mir die Bilderreihen der Wolken an,
Bis sie zerfließen und enthüllen ihre blaue Bahn.

Ich schwebte einsamlich die Welten all hinan,
Entzifferte die Sternoglyphen und die Mondeszeichen
    um den Mann.

Und fragte selbst mich scheu, ob oder wann
Ich einst geboren wurde und gestorben dann?

Mit einem Kleid aus Zweifel war ich angetan,
Das greises Leid geweiht für mich am Zeitrad spann.

Und jedes Bild, das ich von dieser Welt gewann,
Verlor ich doppelt, und auch das was ich ersann.

ICH WEISS

Ich weiß, daß ich bald sterben muß
Es leuchten doch alle Bäume
Nach langersehntem Julikuß—

Fahl werden meine Träume—
Nie dichtete ich einen trüberen Schluß
In den Büchern meiner Reime.

Eine Blume brichst du mir zum Gruß—
Ich liebte sie schon im Keime.
Doch ich weiß, daß ich bald sterben muß.

Mein Odem schwebt über Gottes Fluß—
Ich setze leise meinen Fuß
Auf den Pfad zum ewigen Heime.

DEVOTION

I keep the rows of pictures in the clouds in view
Until they flow apart and show their path of blue.

Up toward the universe I floated lonely on
Deciphered the staroglyphs and signs on the
    man in the moon.

And even shyly asked myself, both if and when
I had been born sometime and then had died again?

I was attired in garments made of doubt
That hoary pain for me on time's great wheel spun out.

And every picture of the world that I could find
Doubly I lost, even those made in my mind.

I KNOW

I know I must soon die
For all the trees are set aglow
After the kiss, long longed for, of July—

Pale and paler my dreams grow—
In the volumes of my rhymes
Never a gloomier end I know.

You picked a flower to bring your greeting by—
I loved it even as a seed below.
But I know I must soon die.

My breath is hovering above God's flow—
Homeward to forever, I
Softly set my foot to go.

HERBST

Ich pflücke mir am Weg das letzte Tausendschön. . . .
Es kam ein Engel mir mein Totenkleid zu nähen—
Denn ich muß andere Welten weiter tragen.

Das ewige Leben *dem*, der viel von Liebe weiß zu sagen.
Ein Mensch der *Liebe* kann nur auferstehen!
Haß schachtelt ein! wie hoch die Fackel auch mag schlagen.

Ich will dir viel viel Liebe sagen—
Wenn auch schon kühle Winde wehen,
In Wirbeln sich um Bäume drehen,
Um Herzen, die in ihren Wiegen lagen.

Mir ist auf Erden weh geschehen. . . .
Der Mond gibt Antwort dir auf deine Fragen.
Er sah verhängt mich auch an Tagen,
Die zaghaft ich beging auf Zehen.

AUTUMN

I pick beside the path the last daisy that unfurls. . . .
To sew my burial shroud an angel came to me—
For I must go on bearing other worlds.

Eternal life to *him* who can say much of love.
A being of *love* will rise most certainly!
Hate boxes in! High though the torch may flare above.

Much love, much love to you I'll say—
Even if there should blow a chilly breeze,
Turning in whirls about the trees,
Around the hearts that in their cradles lay.

On earth much hurt was done to me. . . .
The moon will answer questions you may raise.
He saw me even veiled on days
Which I traversed on tiptoe, timidly.

DEM VERKLARTEN

Ach bitter und karg war mein Brot,
Verblichen—
Das Gold meiner Wangen Bernstein.

In die Höhlen schleiche ich
Mit den Pantern
In der Nacht.

So bange mir in der Dämmerung Weh . . .
Legen sich auch schlafen
Die Sterne auf meine Hand.

Du staunst über ihr Leuchten—
Doch fremd dir die Not
Meiner Einsamkeit.

Es erbarmen sich auf den Gassen
Die wilden Tiere meiner.
Ihr Heulen endet in Liebesklängen.

Du aber wandelst entkommen dem Irdischen
Um den Sinai lächelnd verklärt—
Fremdfern vorüber meiner Welt.

TO MY TRANSFIGURED FRIEND

Ah bitter and scanty was my bread,
Pale as death—
The gold of my cheeks was amber.

Into the caves I creep
With panthers
In the night.

So anxious I in the twilight's sorrow . . .
Even if the stars lie down
On my hand to sleep.

You're surprised by their gleam—
But the pain of my loneliness
Is a stranger to you.

Wild animals in the streets
Take pity upon me.
Their howling ends in sounds of love.

You, though, wander freed of such earthly things
Around Sinai, smiling, radiant—
Strange, far past my world.

EIN LIEBESLIED

Komm zu mir in der Nacht—wir schlafen engverschlungen.
Müde bin ich sehr, vom Wachen einsam.
Ein fremder Vogel hat in dunkler Frühe schon gesungen,
Als noch mein Traum mit sich und mir gerungen.

Es öffnen Blumen sich vor allen Quellen
Und färben sich mit deiner Augen Immortellen. . . .

Komm zu mir in der Nacht auf Siebensternenschuhen
Und Liebe eingehüllt spät in mein Zelt.
Es steigen Monde aus verstaubten Himmelstruhen.

Wir wollen wie zwei seltene Tiere liebesruhen
Im hohen Rohre hinter dieser Welt.

A LOVE SONG

Come to me in the night—close interlaced we'll lie.
I'm lonely from waking and tired as I can be.
Already in early darkness a strange bird has given cry,
While yet my dream did battle with itself and me.

At the springs the opening flowers take on the hue
Of your eyes' periwinkle blue. . . .

Come to me in the night in seven-star shoes
And robed in love, and late into my tent.
Out of the dusty trunks of heaven bright moons suffuse.

Like two rare animals we'll love-rest, curled
Here in the high reeds behind the world.

IN MEINEM SCHOSSE

In meinem Schoße
Schlafen die dunkelen Wolken—
Darum bin ich so traurig, du Holdester.

Ich muß deinen Namen rufen
Mit der Stimme des Paradiesvogels
Wenn sich meine Lippen bunt färben.

Es schlafen schon alle Bäume im Garten—
Auch der nimmermüde
Vor meinem Fenster—

Es rauscht der Flügel des Geiers
Und trägt mich durch die Lüfte
Bis über dein Haus.

Meine Arme legen sich um deine Hüften,
Mich zu spiegeln
In deines Leibes Verklärtheit.

Lösche mein Herz nicht aus—
Du den Weg findest—
Immerdar.

IN MY LAP

In my lap
Sleep the darkening clouds—
Wherefore I am so sad, sweet man.

I must cry out your name
With the voice of the Bird of Paradise,
When my lips flush brightly.

All the trees of the garden have gone to sleep—
The tireless one too
In front of my window—

The wing of the vulture rushes
Bearing me through the winds
Above your home.

My arms clasp round your hips
To seek reflection
In your body's refulgent light.

Don't extinguish my heart—
You'll find the way—
Forever.

DEM HOLDEN

Ich taumele über deines Leibes goldene Wiese,
Es glitzern auf dem Liebespfade hin die Demantkiese
Und auch zu meinem Schoße
Führen bunterlei Türkise.

Ich suchte ewig dich—es bluten meine Füße—
Ich löschte meinen Durst mit deines Lächelns Süße.
Und fürchte doch, daß sich das Tor
Des Traumes schließe.

Ich sende dir, eh ich ein Tropfen frühes Licht genieße,
In blauer Wolke eingehüllte Grüße
Und von der Lippe abgepflückte eben erst erblühte Küsse.
Bevor ich schwärmend in den Morgen fließe.

TO THE DEAR ONE

Over your body's golden fields I run and play;
The diamond gravel glitters all along love's way,
And likewise to my womb
Turquoise of many colors leads the way.

I searched for you forever—with bleeding feet—
I fed my hunger on your smile's red sweet.
And yet I am afraid the dream
Will bar its gate.

I send you, before I drink a drop of dawn,
My greetings with blue clouds around them drawn,
And just-bloomed kisses plucked off of my lips
Before I flow enraptured toward the morn.

DIE UNVOLLENDETE

Es ist so dunkel heut am Heiligen Himmel. . . .
Ich und die Abendwolken suchen nach dem Mond—
Wo beide wir einst vor dem Erdenleben,
Schon nahe seiner Leuchtewelt gewohnt.

Darum möcht ich mit dir mich unlösbar verweben—
Ich hab so Angst um Mitternacht!
Es schreckt ein Traum mich aus vergangenem Leben
An den ich gar nicht mehr gedacht.

Ich pflückte mir so gern nach banger Nacht
Vom Berg der Frühe lichtgefüllte Reben.
Doch hat die Finsternis mich umgebracht—
Geopfert deinem Wunderleben.

Und es verblutet, was du mir,
Ich dir gegeben,
Und auch das bunte Sternenzeichen
Unserer engverknüpften Hand,
Das Pfand!!

Und neben mir und dein—
Auf meinem Herzen süßgemalt enthobnem Sein
—Tröstet mich ein Fremder übermannt.

Ihm mangelt an der Ouvertüre süßem Tand
Streichelnder Flüsterspiele seiner Triebe,
Verherrlichend den keuschen Liebeskelch der Liebe.

THE UNPERFECTED WOMAN

It is so dark today in the Sacred Skies. . . .
I and the evening clouds look for the moon—
Where both of us once, before our earthly lives,
Lived close to the gleaming world that it illumed.

That's why I'd like, indissolubly, to weave myself to you.
At midnight my fears are overwrought!
A dream strikes terror in me, from a life long through,
Of which I had no longer thought.

After a frightened night I loved to gather,
In the vineyards of the dawn, grapes full of light.
But I have been murdered by the dreadful darkness
To your miraculous life a sacrifice.

And what you gave me, and I you,
Has bled to death
And, too, the colorful starry signs
Of our close-twining hand,
Our pledge's band!!

And next to me and your
Suspended being, sweet-painted on my heart,
—A stranger reconciles me thus outmanned.

He's lacking in the overture's sweet, trifling art,
Caressing whisper-games of his desires,
That glorify the chaste cup of love's fires.

AN APOLLON

Es ist am Abend im April.
Der Käfer kriecht ins dichte Moos.
Er hat *so* Angst—die Welt *so* groß!

Die Wirbelwinde hadern mit dem Leben,
Ich halte meine Hände still ergeben
Auf meinem frommbezwungenen Schoß.

Ein Engel spielte sanft auf blauen Tasten,
Langher verklungene Phantasie.
Und alle Bürde meiner Lasten,
Verklärte und entschwerte sie.

Jäh tut mein sehr verwaistes Herz mir weh—
Blutige Fäden spalten seine Stille.
Zwei Augen blicken wund durch ihre Marmorhülle
In meines pochenden Granates See.

Er legte Brand an meines Herzens Lande—
Nicht mal sein Götterlächeln
Ließ er mir zum Pfande.

TO APOLLO

It is April in the evening.
The beetle creeps his mossy paths;
He's *so* afraid—the world's *so* vast!

And Life is a-quarrel with the whirlwinds' commotion.
I fold my hands in still devotion
On knees by piety held fast.

Softly an angel played upon blue keys
Long-faded fantasies,
Which weightlessness and radiance bestowed
On all the burden of my load.

My very orphaned heart abruptly aches—
When bloody threads cut up its quietude.
Two eyes look painfully through its marble hood
Into my pulsating pomegranate's lakes.

He put the torch to my heart's landing place—
And didn't even leave as pledge
That godlike smile upon his face.

AN MICH

Meine Dichtungen, deklamiert, verstimmen die Klaviatür meines Herzens. Wenn es noch Kinder wären, die auf meinen Reimen tastend meinetwegen klimperten. (Bitte nicht weitersagen!) Ich sitze noch heute sitzengeblieben auf der untersten Bank der Schulklasse, wie einst . . . Doch mit spätem versunkenem Herzen: 1000 und 2-jährig, dem Märchen über den Kopf gewachsen.

Ich schweife umher! Mein Kopf fliegt fort wie ein Vogel, liebe Mutter. Meine Freiheit soll mir niemand rauben,—sterb ich am Wegrand wo, liebe Mutter, kommst du und trägst mich hinauf zum blauen Himmel. Ich weiß, dich rührte mein einsames Schweben und das spielende Ticktack meines und meines teuren Kindes Herzen.

TO ME

My poems, declaimed, untune the keyboard of my heart. If only it were children who picked and clinked around on my rhymes—as far as I care. (Don't tell anyone else!) Here I sit still today, having flunked the grade, on the hindmost bench of the class—as once before . . . But with a late, sunken heart! 1000 and 2 years old, the fairy tale now outgrown.

I'm wandering! My head flies away like a bird, dear mother. Nobody will steal my freedom—if I die somewhere by the side of the road, dear mother, you'll come and carry me up to blue heaven. I know that my lonely floating touched you and the playful ticktock of mine and my dear child's heart.

Identifications

Barbarian, The: Gottfried Benn, see p. 21.

Baum, Peter: (1869–1916) Like Lasker-Schüler a native of Elberfeld. Author of verse and fiction influenced by Edgar A. Poe and E. T. A. Hoffmann. A member of Peter Hille's circle, see p. 16. Died in World War I.

Daniel Jesus Paul: See Paul Leppin, author of the novel *Daniel Jesus*.

Duke of Leipzig: See Hans Adalbert von Maltzahn.

Davringhausen, Heinrich Maria: (1894–   ) Sculptor, painter, and lithographer of biblical subjects, figures, landscapes, still lifes, and portraits. Portraits masklike, more types than individuals. Style change from expressionist distortion to new objectivity.

Ehrenbaum-Degele, Hans: (1889–1915) Editor with Paul Zech of the periodical *The New Pathos (Das neue Pathos)* during the years 1913–14. Author of a play and verses. Killed in Russia during World War I.

Giselheer: Gottfried Benn, see p. 21.

Grosz, Georg: (1893–1959) Painter and graphic artist from Berlin, particularly known for political satire directed against capitalism, militarism, the bourgeoisie, and German society's moral decay. Moved to New York in 1932. Participated in American social realism.

King of Bohemia: See Paul Leppin.

Kestenberg, Leo: (1882–1962) Pianist, professor of music in Berlin, and active in cultural education for the Socialist party. As an official in the Prussian Ministry of Culture, he introduced important reforms in music education in the schools. After 1933, exile in Prague, Paris, and Israel.

Leppin, Paul: (1878–1945) Writer of tales, plays, lyrics, and novels, the latter including *Daniel Jesus* (1905). Professionally an official in Prague.

Marc, Franz: (1880–1916) One of the internationally best-known German expressionist painters, especially for the "Blue Horses" and other animal subjects. Later nonobjective style. Born in Munich; died in World War I.

Monk, The: All poems to the "Monk" are dedicated to "F. J.," perhaps Franz Jung, contributor to the periodical *Aktion* and author of the novel *Sacrifice (Opferung)*.

Sascha: See Johannes Holzmann, p. 6.

Schmidtbonn, Wilhelm: (1876–1952) Playwright, fiction writer, and lyric poet, born in Bonn. War correspondent in World War I. His first drama marked the transition from naturalism to neoromanticism in Germany. Depicted landscape and people of the Rhineland.

Senna Hoy: Johannes Holzmann, see p. 6.

Steger, Milly: (1881–1948) Sculptress of wood and stone in Berlin. Studied in Paris with Rodin and Maillol. Known for figures of girls, portrait busts, and sculpture on public buildings in Hagen. Teacher at the Women Artists' Club in Berlin.

Trakl, Georg: (1887–1914) Austrian lyric poet, one of the most significant poets of the expressionist movement. Author of melancholy but sonorous poems of a basically elegiac and pessimistic mood. Died of an overdose of drugs while a medic in World War I.

Tristan: See Hans Ehrenbaum-Degele.

306 Identifications

Trübner, Alice: (1875–1916) Born in England; youth in Frankfurt. Painted heads in a monumental relief style, then landscapes, still life, and portraits.

Werfel, Franz: (1890–1945) Expressionist lyric poet from Prague. Proclaimer of the renewal of mankind. Also a dramatist and later particularly known as an historical, religious, and utopian novelist, especially as author of *The Song of Bernadette* and *Star of the Unborn*.

Else Lasker-Schüler Select Bibliography

A bibliography of works by Lasker-Schüler published during her lifetime and after, a comprehensive listing of her artistic works, and a more extensive coverage of critical articles published prior to 1978, will be found in Sigrid Bauschinger, *Else Lasker-Schüler: Ihr Werk und ihre Zeit* (Heidelberg, 1980). See also the extensive bibliographies in Dieter Bänsch, *Else Lasker-Schüler: Zur Kritik eines etablierten Bildes* (Stuttgart, 1971), and in Margarete Kupper, *Die Weltanschauung Else Lasker-Schülers in ihren poetischen Selbstzeugnissen* (Diss., Würzburg, 1963).

I. Select Works and Letters by Else Lasker-Schüler Published since 1950

"Ein Brief an Thomas Mann." *Bulletin of the Leo Baeck Institute* (Tel Aviv) 11, no. 42 (1968): 259–64.
Briefe an Karl Kraus. Astrid Gehlhoff-Claes, ed. Cologne-Berlin, n.d.
Briefe, I: Lieber gestreifter Tiger. Margarete Kupper, ed. Munich, 1969.
Briefe, II: Wo ist unser buntes Theben. M. Kupper, ed. Munich, 1969.
Dichtungen und Dokumente: Gedichte, Prosa, Schauspiele, Briefe, Zeugnis und Erinnerung. Ernst Ginsberg, ed. Munich, 1951.
"Drei Briefe." *Bulletin of the Leo Baeck Inst.* 8, no. 29 (1965): 1–6.
Else Lasker-Schüler: Eine Einführung in ihr Werk und eine Auswahl. Werner Kraft, ed. Wiesbaden, 1951.
Else Lasker-Schüler: Hebrew Ballads and Other Poems, translated by Audri Durchslag and Jeanette Litman-Demeestère. Philadelphia, 1980.
Gedichte und Prosa: Eine Auswahl. Nachwort von Friedrich Mickwitz. Weimar, 1967.
Gesammelte Werke, I: Gedichte, 1902–1943. Friedhelm Kemp, ed. Munich, 1959.
———, *II: Prosa und Schauspiele*. Friedhelm Kemp, ed. Munich, 1962.
———, *III: Verse und Prosa aus dem Nachlaß*. Werner Kraft, ed. Munich, 1961.
Gesichte: Essays und andere Geschichten. (Reprint of the edition of 1913.) Nendeln/Liechtenstein, 1973.
Das Hebräerland. Munich, 1981.
Ichundich: Eine theatralische Tragödie. Munich, 1980.
Mein Herz: Ein Liebesroman mit Bildern. (Reprint of the edition of 1912.) Nendeln/Liechtenstein, 1973.
Mein Herz: Ein Liebesroman mit Bildern und wirklich lebenden Menschen. Mit Zeichnungen der Autorin aus der Ausgabe von 1912. Frankfurt, 1976.
Der Prinz von Theben: Ein Geschichtenbuch. (Reprint of the edition of 1914.) Nendeln/Liechtenstein, 1973.
Sämtliche Gedichte. Friedhelm Kemp, ed. Munich, 1977.
Was soll ich hier? Exilbriefe an Salman Schocken. Sigrid Bauschinger, ed. Heidelberg, 1981.
Die Wolkenbrücke: Ausgewählte Briefe. Margarete Kupper, ed. Munich, 1972.
Die Wupper—Arthur Aronymus und seine Väter. Munich, 1965.
Die Wupper: Schauspiel in 5 Aufzügen, Mit Dokumenten zur Entstehungs- und Wirkungsgeschichte und einem Nachwort von Fritz Martini. Stuttgart, 1977.

II. Select Secondary Literature on Lasker-Schüler and Her Work

Ahl, Herbert. "Else Lasker-Schüler." *Welt und Wort* 18 (1962): 277–80.
Aker, E. *Untersuchungen der Lyrik Else Lasker-Schülers*. Diss., Munich, 1956.
Auer, Leopold. "Mein blaues Klavier: Zum 25. Todestag Else Lasker-Schülers." *Literatur und Kritik* 5, no. 42 (1970): 113–17.
Bänsch, Dieter. *Else Lasker-Schüler: Zur Kritik eines etablierten Bildes*. Stuttgart, 1971.
Baldrian, Brigitte. *Form und Struktur der Bildlichkeit bei Else Lasker-Schüler*. Diss., Freiburg i. Breisgau, 1926.
Bauschinger, Sigrid. *Else Lasker-Schüler: Ihr Werk und ihre Zeit*. Heidelberg, 1980.
_____. "Else Lasker-Schüler in ihren Briefen." *Neue Rundschau* 81 (1970): 366–74.
_____. *Die Symbolik des Mütterlichen im Werke Else Lasker-Schülers*. Stuttgart, 1960. (Diss., Frankfurt/M., 1960.)
Beck, Evelyn Torton. "Franz Kafka and Else Lasker-Schüler: Alienation and Exile, A Psychocultural Comparison." *Perspectives on Contemporary Literature* 1, no. ii (1975): 31–47.
Ben-Chorin, Schalom. "Else Lasker-Schüler." In his *Zwiesprache mit Martin Buber: Ein Erinnerungsbuch*, pp. 75–81. Munich, 1966.
_____. "Else Lasker-Schüler und Israel." *Literatur und Kritik*, no. 105 (1976): 291–97.
_____. "Else Lasker-Schüler zum 100. Geburtstag." *Almanach für Literatur und Theologie* 3 (1969): 178–92.
_____. "Jussuf in Jerusalem." In *Ein Buch . . .*, edited by Michael Schmid, pp. 55–69. Wuppertal, 1969.
_____. "Prinz Jussuf in Jerusalem." In *Else Lasker-Schüler, Dichtungen und Dokumente*, edited by Ernst Ginsberg, pp. 582–90. Munich, 1951.
Benn, Gottfried. "Else Lasker-Schüler." In *Gottfried Benn: Gesammelte Werke*, edited by Dieter Wellershoff, 4:1101–4. Wiesbaden, 1968.
Berg, Herbert. "The Child Faces Crisis: A Study of Thematic Relationships in the Early Poetry of Else Lasker-Schüler and in the *Menschheitsdämmerung* Anthology." *Dissertation Abstracts International* 36 (1975): 298A–99A.
Bienek, Horst. "Else Lasker-Schüler." In *Triffst du nur das Zauberwort: Stimmen von heute zur deutschen Lyrik*, edited by Jürgen Petersen, pp. 186–95. Frankfurt, 1961.
Blei, Franz. "Der Laskerschüler." In his *Das große Bestiarium: Schriften in Auswahl*, p. 46. Munich, 1960.
Bleyl, Hansjoachim. "Geschichte um die 'Wupper' in der Schaubühne." *Neue Deutsche Hefte* 23 (1976): 646–50.
Blumenthal, Bernhardt. *Aspects of Love in the Life and Works of Else Lasker-Schüler*. Diss., Princeton, 1965.
_____. "The Play Element in the Poetry of Else Lasker-Schüler." *German Quarterly* 43 (1970): 571–76.
Carr, G. J. "Zu den Briefen Else Lasker-Schülers an Karl Kraus." *Literatur und Kritik* 5, no. 49 (1970): 549–56.
Cohn, Hans W. *Else Lasker-Schüler: The Broken World*. Cambridge, 1974. (Anglica Germanica, Series 2.)
David, Claude. "Karl Kraus—Else Lasker-Schüler." *Etudes Germaniques* 15, no. 4 (1960): 364–68.
Domdey, Horst. *Frühe und späte Lyrik Else Lasker-Schülers: Vergleichende Untersuchungen zu Gehalt und Rhythmus*. Berlin, 1964. (Diss., Berlin, 1964.)
Dorst, Tankred. "Szene für Else." *Emuna* 4 (1969): 23.
Dürrson, Werner. "Der Seltsamsaft: Zu Else Lasker-Schülers Einfluß auf die Lyrik von

Gottfried Benn." In *Denken in Widersprüchen: Korrelarien zur Gottfried-Benn-Forschung*, edited by Wolfgang Peitz, pp. 184–204. Freiburg i. Breisgau, 1971.

Ficker, Ludwig von. "Die religiöse Bedeutung der Dichterin Else Lasker-Schüler." In *Else Lasker-Schüler, Dichtungen und Dokumente*, pp. 606–9. Munich, 1951.

Fischer, Grete. *Dienstboten, Brecht und andere: Zeitgenossen in Prag, Berlin, London*. Olten, Freiburg i. Breisgau, 1966.

Fischer, Heinrich. "Else Lasker-Schüler zum Gedächtnis." In *Else Lasker-Schüler, Dichtungen und Dokumente*, pp. 601–4. Munich, 1951.

Gehlhoff-Claes, Astrid. "Versuch einer biographischen Darstellung." In *Briefe an Karl Kraus*, edited by A. Gehlhoff-Claes, pp. 141–76. Cologne-Berlin, 1959. (Separately printed as Folge 2 of the "Wuppertaler Biographien," 1960.)

Gertner, Meier. "Biblische Spiegelbilder." In *Ein Buch . . .*, edited by Michael Schmid, pp. 166–82. Wuppertal, 1969.

Ginsberg, Ernst. "Else Lasker-Schüler." In his *Abschied*, pp. 153–66. Zurich, 1965.

———. "Es steigen aus verstaubten Himmelstruhen." *Frankfurter Allgemeine Zeitung*, no. 13 (1965).

———, ed. *Else Lasker-Schüler, Dichtungen und Dokumente: Gedichte, Prosa, Schauspiele, Briefe, Zeugnis und Erinnerung*. Munich, 1951.

Goetz, Markete. "Else Lasker-Schüler's Play *Die Wupper*: A Forerunner of Contemporary Drama." *Proceedings of the Pacific Northwest Conference on Foreign Languages, Sixteenth Annual Meeting, April 22–24, 1965*, pp. 101–8.

Goldscheider, Paul. "Wo ich bin, ist es grün." In *Ein Buch . . .*, edited by Michael Schmid, pp. 50–54. Wuppertal, 1969.

Goldstein, Fanni. *Der expressionistische Stilwelle im Werke Else Lasker-Schülers*. Diss., Vienna, 1936.

Gottgetreu, Erich. "Else Lasker-Schüler und 'der Urböse.'" *Emuna* 4 (1969): 246–48.

———. "Näher heran an Else Lasker-Schüler." *Neue Deutsche Hefte* 168 (1980): 797–801.

Grosshut, F. S. "Else Lasker-Schüler in der Emigration." In *Ein Buch . . .*, edited by Michael Schmid, pp. 590–93. Wuppertal, 1969.

Guder, Gotthard. *Else Lasker-Schüler: Deutung ihrer Lyrik*. Siegen, 1966.

———. "Else Lasker-Schüler's Conception of Herself as a Poet." *Orbis Litterarum* 15, no. 3/4 (1960): 184–99.

———. "The Image of the Angel in the Poetry of Else Lasker-Schüler." *Modern Languages* 47 (1966): 98–103.

———. "The Meaning of Colour in Else Lasker-Schüler's Poetry." *German Life and Letters* 15 (1961): 175–87.

———. "The Poetry of Else Lasker-Schüler." *Modern Languages* 43 (1962): 53–60.

———. "The Significance of Love in the Poetry of Else Lasker-Schüler." *German Life and Letters* 18 (1965): 177–88.

Hegglin, Werner. *Else Lasker-Schüler und ihr Judentum*. Zurich, 1966.

Hermlin, Stephan. *Lektüre, 1960–1971*. Frankfurt/M., 1974.

Herzfelde, Wieland. "Else Lasker-Schüler: Begegnungen mit der Dichterin und ihrem Werk." *Sinn und Form* 21 (1969): 1294–325.

———. "Fremd und Nah: Über meinen Briefwechsel und meine Begegnungen mit Else Lasker-Schüler." *Marginalien: Blätter der Pirckheimer Gesellschaft*, no. 18 (1965): 1–7.

———. "Kürzlich vor 60 Jahren." *Sinn und Form* 27 (1975): 371–84.

———. *Zur Sache geschrieben und gesprochen zwischen 18 und 80*. Berlin, 1976.

Heselhaus, Clemens. "Else Lasker-Schülers literarisches Traumspiel." In his *Deutsche Lyrik der Moderne*, pp. 213–28. Düsseldorf, 1961.

Hessing, Jakob. "Else Lasker-Schüler and Her People." *Ariel* 41 (1976): 61–76.

Hirshberg, Jehoash. "Joseph Tal's Homage to Else." *Ariel* 41 (1976): 83–93.
Höltgen, K. J. *Untersuchungen zur Lyrik Else Lasker-Schülers*. Bonn, 1958. (Diss., Bonn, 1955.)
Jais, Agathe. *Else Lasker-Schüler: Die Lyrik der mittleren Schaffensperiode*. Diss., Munich, 1965.
Jung, Cläre M. "Bilder meines Lebens" (Two parts). *Neue Deutsche Literatur*, 19, no. 2 (1971): 114–31; and 20, no. 4 (1972): 109–22.
Kesting, Marianne. "Else Lasker-Schüler und ihr blaues Klavier." *Deutsche Rundschau*, no. 83 (1957): 66–70.
———. "Zur Dichtung Else Lasker-Schülers." *Akzente* 3 (1956): 377–83.
Klotz, Volker. "Das blaue große Bilderbuch mit Sternen." In his *Kurze Kommentare zu Stücken und Gedichten*, pp. 61–70. Darmstadt, 1962.
Klüsener, Erika. *Else Lasker-Schüler in Selbstzeugnissen und Bilddokumenten*. Hamburg, 1980.
———. "Else Lasker-Schüler: Eine Biographie oder ein Werk?" *Dissertation Abstracts International* 40 (1980): 4068A–69A.
Koch, Angelika. *Die Bedeutung des Spiels bei Else Lasker-Schüler im Rahmen von Expressionismus und Manierismus* (Abhandlungen zur Kunst-, Musik- und Literaturwissenschaft, 107). Bonn, 1971.
Kraft, Werner. "Else Lasker-Schüler." In *Juden, Christen, Deutsche*, edited by Hans Jürgen Schulz, pp. 380–88. Stuttgart, 1961.
———. "Erinnerungen an Else Lasker-Schüler." *Hochland* 43, no. 6 (1951): 588–92.
———. *Else Lasker-Schüler: Eine Einführung in ihr Werk und eine Auswahl*. Wiesbaden, 1951.
Kraus, Karl. "Anmerkung zum 'Tibetteppich.'" *Die Fackel* 12, nos. 313–14 (1910): 36.
———. "Der Reim." In *Else Lasker-Schüler, Dichtungen und Dokumente*, edited by Ernst Ginsberg, pp. 570–72. Munich, 1951.
Kunz, Ludwig. "Verse bei Kerzenlicht." In *Ein Buch* . . . , edited by Michael Schmid, pp. 70–72. Wuppertal, 1969.
Kupper, Margarete. "Lebenslauf." In *Else Lasker-Schüler: Sämtliche Gedichte*, edited by Friedhelm Kemp, pp. 291–310. Munich, 1966.
———. "Materialien zu einer kritischen Ausgabe der Lyrik Else Lasker-Schülers." *Jahrbuch der Görres-Gesellschaft, Neue Folge* 4 (1963): 95–190.
———. "Der Nachlaß Else Lasker-Schülers in Jerusalem: Ein Bericht." *Jahrbuch der Görres-Gesellschaft* 9 (1968): 243–83.
———. "Der Nachlaß Else Lasker-Schülers in Jerusalem, II. Verzeichnis der Briefe an Else Lasker-Schüler" (Mit Textabdruck). *Jahrbuch der Görres-Gesellschaft* 10 (1969): 175–230.
———. "Der Nachlaß Else Lasker-Schülers, III. Epistolographie (1): Register der veröffentlichten und der unveröffentlichten Briefe von Else Lasker-Schüler." *Jahrbuch der Görres-Gesellschaft* 11 (1970): 225–83.
———. "Der Nachlaß Else Lasker-Schülers, III. Epistolographie (2): Korrektur der Briefdrucke. Auswahl bisher unveröffentlichter Briefe von Else Lasker-Schüler" (Mit Textpublikationen). *Jahrbuch der Görres-Gesellschaft* 12 (1971): 241–91.
———. *Die Weltanschauung Else Lasker-Schülers in ihren poetischen Selbstzeugnissen*. Diss., Würzburg, 1963.
———. "Wiederentdeckte Texte Else Lasker-Schülers." *Jahrbuch der Görres-Gesellschaft* 5 (1964): 229–63.
———. "Wiederentdeckte Texte, II." *Jahrbuch der Görres-Gesellschaft* 6 (1965): 227–33.

---. "Wiederentdeckte Texte, III. Aus dem Lasker-Schüler-Archiv in Jerusalem." *Jahrbuch der Görres-Gesellschaft* 8 (1967): 175–99.

---. "Ein wiederentdecktes Gedicht von Else Lasker-Schüler." *Germanisch-romanische Monatsschrift*, Neue Folge 13 (1963): 80–91.

---, ed. "*Ichundich*: Nachlaßschauspiel von Else Lasker-Schüler." *Jahrbuch der deutschen Schiller-Gesellschaft* 14 (1970): 24–99.

Laube, Horst. "Nur eine originelle Blüte?" In *Ein Buch . . .* , edited by Michael Schmid, pp. 114–22. Wuppertal, 1969.

Lienau, Marianne. "Anarchie nach innen." In *Ein Buch . . .* , edited by Michael Schmid, pp. 101–11. Wuppertal, 1969.

Lindtberg, Leopold. "So glänzte der Traum des Arthur Aronymus." In *Ein Buch . . .* , edited by Michael Schmid, pp. 73–86. Wuppertal, 1969.

Macht, Richard M. "Motifs of Judaic Mysticism in the Poetry of Else Lasker-Schüler." *Dissertation Abstracts* 29 (1969): 3146A–47A.

Marc, Franz. *Briefe, Aufzeichnungen und Aphorismen*. Berlin, 1920.

Marc, M. *Franz Marc: Botschaften an den Prinzen Jussuf*. Munich, 1954.

Marsch, Edgar. "Else Lasker-Schüler." In *Deutsche Dichter der Moderne: Ihr Leben und Werk*, edited by Benno von Wiese, pp. 365–88. 2nd. ed. Berlin, 1969.

Martini, Fritz. "Else Lasker-Schüler." In his *Was war Expressionismus?* pp. 107–11. Urach, 1948.

---. "Else Lasker-Schüler: Dichtung und Glaube." In *Der deutsche Expressionismus: Formen und Gestalten*, edited by Hans Steffen, pp. 5–24. Göttingen, 1965.

Masini, Ferruccio. *Itinerario sperimentale nella letteratura tedesca*. Parma, 1970.

Meyer, André. "Vorahnungen der Judenkatastrophe bei Heinrich Heine und Else Lasker-Schüler." *Bulletin of the Leo Baeck Institute* 8, no. 29 (1965): 7–27.

Muschg, Walter. "Else Lasker-Schüler." In his *Von Trakl zu Brecht: Dichter des Expressionismus*, pp. 115–48. Munich, 1961.

Nachrichten aus dem Kösel-Verlag. (Sonderheft) *Für Else Lasker-Schüler*. Munich, 1965.

Newton, Robert. "Eye Imagery in Else Lasker-Schüler." *Modern Language Notes* 97 (1982): 694–712.

Otto, Teo. "Ein bergischer Kräher berichtet." In *Ein Buch . . .* , edited by Michael Schmid, pp. 41–49. Wuppertal, 1969.

Paepcke, Lotte. "Else Lasker-Schüler." *Frankfurter Hefte* 16 (1961): 33–40.

Pazi, Margarita. "Else Lasker-Schüler in Jerusalem: Zur Nuancierung einer allgemeinen Meinung." *Deutsche Vierteljahresschrift für Literaturwisseschaft und Geistesgeschichte* 53 (1979): 115–24.

Pörtner, Paul. "Poesie lebte." In *Ein Buch . . .* , edited by Michael Schmid, pp. 183–93. Wuppertal, 1969.

Politzer, Heinz. "The Blue Piano of Else Lasker-Schüler." *Commentary* 9, no. 4 (1950): 336.

---. "Else Lasker-Schüler." In *Expressionismus als Literatur: Gesammelte Studien*, edited by Wolfgang Rothe, pp. 215–32. Bern and Munich, 1969.

Raabe, Paul. "Gottfried Benns Huldigungen an Else Lasker-Schüler. Unbekannte Dokumente des Dichters, 1931–32." In *Gottfried Benn. Den Traum alleine tragen. Texte, Briefe, Dokumente*, edited by Paul Raabe and Max Niedermayer, pp. 61–79. Wiesbaden, 1966.

Radecki, Sigismund von. "Erinnerungen an Else Lasker-Schüler." In *Else Lasker-Schüler: Dichtungen und Dokumente*, edited by Ernst Ginsberg, pp. 575–82. Munich, 1951.

Rosenfeld, Emmy. "Wanderer zwischen den Welten (Else Lasker-Schüler und Franz Werfel)." In *Studi e ricerche di letteratura inglese e americana*, edited by Claudio Gorlier, 2:259–86. Milan, 1969.
Rost, Nico. "Ontmoetingen met Prins Tino van Bagdad." *De Vlaamse Gids* 49 (1965): 331–36.
Schlocker, Georges. "Else Lasker-Schüler." In *Expressionismus: Gestalten einer literarischen Bewegung*, ed. H. Friedmann and O. Mann, pp. 140–54. Heidelberg, 1956.
———. "Exkurs über Else Lasker-Schüler." In *Deutsche Literatur im 20. Jahrhundert*, ed. O. Mann and W. Rothe, vol. 1: 344–57. Bern and Munich, 1967.
Schlösser, Manfred. "Deutsch-jüdische Dichtung des Exils." *Emuna* 3 (1968), 250–65.
Schmid, Michael. "Else Lasker-Schüler. Eine Biographie." In *Ein Buch* . . . , edited by Michael Schmid, pp. 7–40. Wuppertal, 1969.
———, ed. *Else Lasker-Schüler: Ein Buch zum 100. Geburtstag der Dichterin*. Wuppertal, 1969.
———. "Schwierigkeiten mit Arthur Aronymus." *Emuna* 4 (1969): 257–58.
Springmann, Wolfgang. "Else Lasker-Schüler und ihre Wuppertaler Heimat." *Emuna* 4 (1969): 15–22.
———. *Else Lasker-Schüler und Wuppertal: Auswahl und Kommentar von Wolfgang Springmann*, Neue verbesserte Auflage. Wuppertal-Elberfeld, 1965. (Veröffentlichungen der Stadtbibliothek Wuppertal, VI.)
Sturmann, M. "Briefe an Else Lasker-Schüler, zur Einführung." *Bulletin of the Leo Baeck Institute* 2, no. 7 (1959): 162–66.
Sull, Young Suk. "Die Lyrik Else Lasker-Schülers: Stilelemente und Themenkreise." *Dissertation Abstracts International* 41 (1980): 269A.
Thiel, Heinz. "Ich und Ich: Ein versperrtes Werk?" In *Ein Buch* . . . , edited by Michael Schmid, pp. 123–59. Wuppertal, 1969.
Wallmann, Jürgen. "Ein alter Tibetteppich." *Neue Deutsche Hefte* 11, no. 102 (1964): 63–69.
———. "Deutsche Lyrik unter jüdischem Dreigestirn." *Merkur* 20, no. 12 (1966): 1191–94.
———. *Else Lasker-Schüler*. Mühlacker, 1966.
———. "Hommage für Else Lasker-Schüler." In *Ein Buch* . . . , edited by Michael Schmid, pp. 195–204. Wuppertal, 1969.
Webb, Karl E. "Else Lasker-Schüler and Franz Marc: A Comparison." *Orbis Litterarum* 33 (1978): 280–98.
Weidmann, Brigitte. "Else Lasker-Schüler: Zum 25. Todestag am 22.1.1970." *Neue Deutsche Hefte* 17, no. 1 (1970): pp. 18–27.
Weiß, Richard. "Else Lasker-Schüler." *Die Fackel* 13, no. 321/22 (1911): 42–50.
Weissenberger, Klaus. *Zwischen Stein und Stern: Mystische Formgebung in der Dichtung von Else Lasker-Schüler, Nelly Sachs und Paul Celan*. Bern and Munich, 1976.
Wegner, Armin T. "Unser Kaffeehaus oder die Arche." In *Ein Buch* . . . , edited by Michael Schmid, pp. 87–99. Wuppertal, 1969.
Werner, Gerhart. "Tinos großer Bruder." In *Ein Buch* . . . , edited by Michael Schmid, pp. 160–65. Wuppertal, 1969.
Windfuhr, Manfred. *Die unzulängliche Gesellschaft: Rheinische Sozialkritik von Spee bis Böll*. (Mit 13 Abb.). Stuttgart, 1971.
Zimmermann, Inge M. E. "Der Mensch im Spiegel des Tierbildes: Untersuchungen zum Werk Else Lasker-Schülers." *Dissertation Abstracts International* 41 (1980): 2132A–33A.

Index of Poem Titles
(Bold face refers to English text.)

Abdul Antinous, **199**
Abel, **249**
Abraham and Isaac, 41, 49, **251**
After-Pain, 30, **91**
Alice Trübner, 38, **221**
And Look for God, **139**
Antinous, **239**
Arrival, **131**
Autumn, 31, 43, **289**

Baboon Mother Sings Her Baboonlet to Sleep, The, 20, **239**
Ballad (From the Mountains of the Sauerland), 23, 33, **85**
Ballad, 20, **147**
Black Stars, **105**
But Your Brows Are a Storm, 37, **187**

Chaos, 30, 45, **71**
Chased Away, 25, 49, **285**
Christmas, **271**

Damnation, 30, 43, **73**
David and Jonathan, **261**
David and Jonathan, 33, 49, **263**
Departure, **265**
Devotion, **287**
"Dove That Swims in Its Own Blood," 34, **113**
Dream, 111

Elegy, 33, 43, **93**
End of the World, The, 34, 43, **131**
Esther, 49, **263**
Eve, **115**
Evening Song, **271**
Eve's Song, **121**

Fallen Angel, The, 16, 30, **76**
Fear Deep in My Blood, The, 30, 45, **99**
Flight from the World, 44, **57**
Flight of Love, 33, **111**
Fortissimo, 31, 33, 49, **77**
Franz Marc, 23, **235**
Franz Werfel, **215**

Genesis, 49, **273**
Georg Grosz, **223**
Georg Trakl, **219**
Georg Trakl, 49, **219**
God Hear . . . , 43, **269**
Grotesque, 34, **119**
Guilt, 30, **89**

Hagar and Ishmael, **253**
Hans Ehrenbaum-Degele, **159**
Heinrich Maria Davringhausen, **225**
His Blood, 33, **67**
Homesickness, **141**

I Am Sad, 39, **137**
I Hide behind Trees, 22, **171**
I Know, 26, **287**
In My Lap, **295**
Instinct, 30, 33, **59**
In the Beginning (World Scherzo), 43, **101**

Jacob, 40, **255**
Jacob and Esau, **253**
Jerusalem, 42, **275**

Karma, 33, **65**
Knowledge, 33, **107**

Leave-Taking, 9, **193**
Leave-Taking, **203**
Leo Kestenberg, **229**
Listen, 22, **175**
Love Song, A, 20, 40, **151**
Love Song, A, 31, 49, **293**
Love Stars, **105**
Ludwig Hardt, **231**

Mary of Nazareth, **145**
May Rain, **123**
May Roses, **63**
Milly Steger, **227**
Monk, The, **205**
Moses and Joshua, 41, 49, **259**
My Being, **103**
My Blue Piano, 49, **279**

My Child, 19, **237**
My Drama, 33, **175**
My Love Song, **129**
My Love Song, 20, **149**
My Mother, 13, **143**
My People, 41, **247**
My Quiet Song (first version), 13, 34, **125**
My Quiet Song (second version), 13, **241**

O God, 22, **175**
Oh, Your Hands, 22, **163**
Old Spring, 30, 33, 49, **61**
Old Tibetan Rug, An, 21, 35, **137**
Only for You, 22, **179**
Our Battle Song, **117**
Our Love Song, **197**
Our Proud Song, **115**
Overture, **238**

Pablo, **201**
Peter Baum, **217**
Pharaoh and Joseph, 33, 35, 49, **257**
Prayer, 23, 39–40, 49, **243**
Prayer, 43, 46, 49, **281**
Pure Diamond, 22, **167**

Reconciliation, 38, 39, 49, **245**
Royal Will, **87**

Sabaoth, **265**
Sascha, 20, **155**
Savary Le Duc, **195**
Say It Softly, 38–39, **135**
School Days, 34, **119**
Secretly at Night, 38, **213**
Senna Hoy, 20, **157**
Sensual Ecstasy, 30, 31, 33, **65**
Song, A, 49, **211**
Song of Love, A, 20, 49, **153**

Song of the Playmate Prince, The, 22, **169**
Song of Wonder, The, **267**
Spring, 33, 49, **57**
Spring Sorrow, 45, **103**
Styx, **101**
Suicide, 30, **81**

Then, 49, **63**
To Apollo, **301**
To Daniel Jesus Paul, **191**
To Giselheer the Heathen, 22, 39, **165**
To Giselheer the Tiger, 22, **173**
To Me, **303**
To My Child, 19, 43, 49, **227**
To My Transfigured Friend, **291**
To the Barbarian, 22, **181**
To the Barbarian, 22, 49, **183**
To the Dear One, **297**
To the Duke of Leipzig, **185**
To the King of Bohemia, **189**
To the Knight of Gold, 24, **161**
To the Monk, **207**
To the Monk, **209**
To You, **89**
Turned Inward, 22, **177**
Two of Them, The, **97**

Unhappy Hate, 30, **91**
Unperfected Woman, The, **299**

Vagabonds, 30, 33, **95**
Viva!, 33, 49, **64**

Weltschmerz, 30, 34, 49, **73**
Where Might Death Leave My Heart?, **133**
Wilhelm Schmidtbonn, **233**

You Make Me Sad—Listen, **187**
Youth, 45, 49, **83**

Subject Index

Arthur Aronymus and His Fathers, 25
"Arthur Aronymus: The Story of My Father," 12
"Astrology," 38

Bänsch, Dieter, 14–15, 28, 37, 40–41, 43, 46, 48
Ball, Hugo, 9
Baum, Peter, 24, 217, 305
Bauschinger, Sigrid, 14, 20, 26
Beardsley, Aubrey, 9
Becher, Johannes, 17
Ben-Chorin, Schalom, 47
Benn, Gottfried, 5, 8, 10, 21–22, 31–32, 41–42
"Blue" image, 39

"Child among the Months, The," 15
Cirlot, J. E., 38–40
Cleaning Out!, 19
Cohn, Hans, 20, 23, 29, 32, 38–39, 41–42
Collected Poems, 18, 24, 42
Concert, 15, 25, 27, 40, 43–44, 46

Däubler, Theodor, 3, 13, 24
Dehmel, Richard, 13, 24

Ehrenbaum-Degele, Hans, 19, 24, 42, 159, 305
Ehrenstein, Albert, 24

Fischer, Grete, 31

Gehlhoff-Claes, Astrid, 18–19
George, Stefan, 13, 34, 46–47
Ginsberg, Ernst, 42
Giselheer the Barbarian, 22
Goethe, J. W., 9, 21, 31
"Gold" image, 39–40
Grosz, Georg, 24, 305
Guder, Gotthart, 39

Hart, Julius, 15
Hauptmann, Gerhart, 9
Hebrew Ballads, 24, 40–42

Heine, Heinrich, 48
Hennings, Emmy, 9
Heselhaus, Clemens, 22, 49
Hesse, Hermann, 16
Heym, Georg, 7, 17
Hille, Peter, 3, 10, 15–16, 20, 31, 38, 41
Hiller, Kurt, 19, 32
Hoddis, Jakob van, 7
Hofmannsthal, Hugo von, 13, 20, 23, 47
Holzmann, Johannes, 6, 31–32

I and I, 26
Ibsen, Henrik, 12

Jacometti, Bettina, 9
Jesus, 38, 41–42
Joseph, 13, 24, 44
Jussuf of Egypt, 8, 24, 33

Kissing, Jeanette. *See* Schüler, Jeanette Kissing
Knight of Gold, To the, 24
Kokoschka, Oskar, 19, 24
Kraft, Werner, 23
Kraus, Karl, 3, 14, 18–21, 24, 31, 43
Kupper, Margarete, 24, 27

Land of the Hebrews, 26
Lasker, Berthold, 14
Lasker, Emanuel, 3, 21
Lasker, Paul, 14, 19, 21, 24–25
Laube, Horst, 28
Leppin, Paul, 24, 305
Levin, Georg (*see* Herwarth Walden)
Lienau, Marianne, 28, 47–48
Loos, Alfred, 24

Malik: An Imperial Story, The, 5, 22–24 passim
Maltzahn, Hans Adalbert von, 24, 42
Mann, Thomas, 8, 35
Marc, Franz, 3, 5, 19, 22–23, 235, 305
Martini, Fritz, 27, 35, 41
Muschg, Walter, 38–39
My Blue Piano, 26, 27, 43
"My Devotion," 44

My Heart: A Love Novel with Pictures and Really Living People, 18, 23
My Miracles: Poems, 18, 35, 37

New Community, 15
Nietzsche, Friedrich, 13, 23
Nights of Tino of Baghdad, The, 14, 17–18, 26

Otto, Katharina, 19

Parallelismus membrorum, 35
Perotti, Berto, 25
Peter Hille Book, The, 16, 18
Pörtner, Paul, 48–49
"Poor Children of Rich People," 28
Prince of Thebes, 7–8, 18
Prince of Thebes, The, 23, 26, 33

Radecki, Sigismund von, 32, 41
Reeck, Emerich, 11–12
Rilke, R. M., 23, 41
Rouan, Alcibiades de, 14, 32

Sascha, 6
Schlocker, Georges, 38–39, 48–49
Schüler, Aaron, 12

Schüler, Anna, 13
Schüler, Jeanette Kissing, 12–13
Schüler, Paul, 13
Senna Hoy, 6, 32, 42
Seventh Day, The, 17–18, 33–34
Sonnemann, Leopold, 12
Stadler, Ernst, 17
"Star" image, 37–38
Sturm, Der, 17–18
Styx, 14, 17–18, 23, 31–32, 34, 49

Tino of Baghdad, 7–8, 16
Toller, Ernst, 24
Trakl, Georg, 3, 7, 17, 23–24, 48, 219, 305

Visions: Essays and Other Stories, 18, 38

Walden, Herwarth, 11, 17–18, 31, 44
Wallmann, Jürgen, 12
Wegner, Armin T., 8
Werfel, Franz, 17, 24, 215, 306
Werner, Gerhart, 16
Wilhelm, Kurt, 26
Wodtke, F. W., 22
Wupper, The, 18, 24

Zech, Paul, 19, 24

www.ingramcontent.com/pod-product-compliance
Lightning Source LLC
Chambersburg PA
CBHW021802220426
43662CB00006B/157